CONCILIUM

Religion in the Eighties

CONCILIUM

Concilium 151 (1/1982): Sociology of Religion

THE CHURCH AND RACISM

Edited by

Gregory Baum

and

John Coleman

English Language Editor
Marcus Lefébure

T. & T. CLARK LTD.
Edinburgh

THE SEABURY PRESS
New York

January 1982
T. & T. Clark Ltd., 36 George Street, Edinburgh EH2 2LQ
ISBN: 0 567 30031 5

The Seabury Press, 815 Second Avenue, New York, N.Y. 10017
ISBN: 0 8164 2382 2

Library of Congress Catalog Card No.:

Printed in Scotland by William Blackwood & Sons Ltd., Edinburgh

Concilium: Monthly except July and August
Subscriptions 1982: UK and Rest of the World £27·00, postage and handling included; USA and Canada, all applications for subscriptions and enquiries about *Concilium* should be addressed to, The Seabury Press, 815 Second Avenue, New York, NY 10017, USA.

CONTENTS

Editorial

THIS IS the first issue of *Concilium* to deal with the topic of racism. This fact alone reveals how little importance theologians have attached to the topic. In the past, the Christian churches were identified with the colonial expansion of the western powers and hence approved, without much reflection, of the subordination of colonised peoples, the contempt entertained for non-western cultures, and the economic exploitation of the colonial territories. Few Christians opposed this trend. Only recently, only since the break-down of colonialism, have the churches begun to change their minds and theologians paid critical attention to the sin of racism. Theological reflection is still rudimentary.

After World War II, Christian theologians were willing to confront more directly one particular form of racism, namely the hatred of Jews or anti-Semitism. Reflecting on the mass murder of European Jewry by the Nazi conquerors, the Church examined its own heritage of anti-Jewish teaching, legislation and sentiment. While the Christian tradition was in no sense the creator of Nazi racism—Nazi racism in fact turned against Christianity because of its Jewish roots—the Church's teaching of contempt for Jews and Jewish religion did produce a hostile imagination and symbols of negations which in our century helped Nazi policy gain approval by so many in so short a time. According to this teaching of contempt, the Church has replaced the old Israel, which was now discarded and the object of divine wrath. Jewish religion had fallen into sin: it was a way of blindness, a prison house. The Jews stood under the shadow of death. Since Auschwitz, the churches have been moved to repentance. Thanks to the effort of many theologians and the approval of the church boards and church councils, great efforts have been made to correct catechisms and books of religious instruction and formulate the message of salvation in Christ, without at the same time negating Jewish existence.

The present issue of *Concilium* deals with another form of racism, namely white racism against people of colour. There is also racism among non-white peoples. M. Dhavamony and H. Erlinghagen refer to this in their reports. But since white racism is a universal phenomenon and closely linked to the colonial age and indirectly to the Christian churches during that period, it is white racism that raises a question of primary importance for theology. It is white racism that demands resolute action on the part of the churches. The present issue is only a beginning. Part I presents articles of a more general kind that help the reader to understand the phenomenon of racism and the Christian reaction to it, and Part II offers reports on the Church and racism from several different parts of the world. It is too early to develop a systematic theology for the overcoming of racism, even though this issue contains many important elements for such a theology.

One of the great problems in the overcoming of racism is that the Scriptures themselves are not free of ambiguity. They can be read in a way that legitimates existing racism. The Scriptures can also be read in ways that demand the overcoming of racism and reveal the coming of God's reign in the reconciliation of nations, peoples and races. C. Felder deals with this ambiguity in his article. It is important to realise, however, that cultural oppression and contemptuous feelings for outsiders cannot be equated with racism as a political philosophy. A. Davies shows that racism as an ideology with political and cultural purposes, was the product of the nineteenth century. It is here that we find the ancestor of Nazi racism and of contemporary forms of racism linked to right wing political movements.

Of great practical and theoretical interest is the radical Christian reaction to racist culture and racist religion in Black Theology, produced in the 1960s by Black theologians in the United States. Black theology began as a magnificent counter-statement. Against the hidden presupposition that God was white, pervasive in the dominant culture and the white churches, Black theologians asserted that the God of the churches did not exist at all. God was in fact black. Relying on the apocalyptic themes in the Scriptures, they proclaimed the inversion of the sinful society so that the last shall be the first and the first last. Since the 1960s, Black Theology has moved away from the apocalyptic mood. It has become more systematic, more attentive to the universal Church, more ready to envisage reconciliation with white Christian congregations if they are ready for repentance and conversion. This is the topic of D. Robert's article. The apocalyptic style of the early Black Theology should not too easily be forgotten. For it will return if the churches entertain the idea that their own racism can be overcome by a few kind words and a few practical gestures. Since racism carries with it symbols of negation of the peoples deemed inferior, and since this symbolism operates in people's imagination and their unconscious, churches can free themselves from racism only through a profound catharsis, only through suffering, confusion, and conversion affecting the majority of their members.

What positive contributions have Christians made to the overcoming of racism? Is there some good news? R.-H. Guerrand gives us a brief summary of the Catholic Church's doctrinal opposition to racism. He deals mainly with papal teaching. Some of the concrete actions against racism taken today by the Catholic Church and other Christian churches in various regions, are spelled out in the reports collected in Part II of this issue. J. Brosseder gives an account of the World Council of Churches' struggle against racism, a bold and prophetic enterprise. The WCC has been willing to become controversial in western society. One point this issue of *Concilium* brings out is that there is no way of fighting racism today unless one is willing to become controversial. There is no smooth, gradual, sweet entry into freedom. Catharsis demands a price. For the white churches, heirs of the colonial order, there is no entry into salvation save through some sort of death and resurrection.

An important theoretical contribution to the struggle against racism is R. Siebert's article, which applies the wisdom of Critical Theory, more precisely of Christian Critical Theory, to the phenomenon of racism. Siebert tries to uncover the anthropological foundation for both unity and difference among peoples and races. We must recognise a double need, the need to stress identity and differentiation and the need to emphasise unity and integration. The need for identity non-dialectically affirmed sometimes tempts even noble souls into the blindness of racism, just as the need for integration in and by itself gives rise to a vision of unity that implies the subordination of all to the hegemony of a single people, or the assimilation of the many and hence their virtual disappearance. Siebert shows how this dialectic of unity-in-difference is distorted further by people's material interest, political and economic, and how, therefore, the struggle against racism must insert itself in the reconstruction of the material basis of civilisation. Of theoretical importance is also E. Dussel's report from Latin America, which understands racism and the effort to overcome it from a world historical perspective.

Part II presents reports on the Church and racism from various parts of the world. Each report is different: each concentrates on different aspects of a common struggle, each pursues a different line of thought. Together they reveal that the Church's struggle against racism is only at the beginning. They reveal, moreover, that racism is not a spiritual problem that can be overcome by a change of heart alone; it is a problem linked to the material interests of economic advantage and political domination. The reports bring out that if the churches want to overcome racism, they will have to pay a high price for this. Since racism touches the roots of our collective egotism, the struggle against it is inevitably a radical undertaking. Christians engaged in it will, like the WCC, become controversial.

GREGORY BAUM
JOHN COLEMAN

PART I

Racism and the Christian Churches

Rudolf Siebert

The Phenomenon of Racism

THE PURPOSE of this discourse is to critically explore the modern phenomenon of racism in the framework of historical and dialectical anthropology.[1] This anthropological discourse, which seeks to trace the dialectical development of the human races, must ultimately be understood as future-oriented remembrance, of the horrible suffering and deaths of innumerable innocent victims of religious or secular racist movements on all continents. This concretely Utopian anamnesis of the bloody terror of racism is connected with the practical intent of qualitative personal, social and cultural change, which will make racism (which has so often helped stabilise antagonistic liberal and advanced capitalistic and socialistic societies) unnecessary.[2]

1. RACIAL DIFFERENTIATION AND RACIST PARANOIA

Positive physical and cultural anthropology define race scientifically as a major division of humankind with distinctive hereditary, transmissible physical characteristics, e.g., Negroid, Mongoloid, Caucasoid, etc.[3] Scientifically, race is a breeding group with gene organisation differing from that of the other intraspecific groups. Dialectical anthropology sees race not (as do fascists) as immediately the naturally particular, but rather as the reduction of humankind to that which is natural, to mere power.[4] Race today, however, is the self-assertion of the bourgeois individual who is fully integrated into the barbarous collective. Contrary to the positive and dialectical anthropology of race, racism is the false consciousness of a dominant race concerning itself and dominated races. It is not scientific concern with human races, their differences, interrelationships and conflicts, but a very emotional and passionate ideology. Racism is the rationalisation of the irrational power-structure in which one race instrumentalises, exploits and sometimes even annihilates others; it is the mere appearance necessary for the equilibration of race superiority in contradictory liberal and advanced capitalistic and socialistic societies.[5] Since the ideology of racism is, in reality, nothing more than the systematic distortion of the anthropology of race in the interest of racial dominance, the first step against racism must be scientific clarification of race differences and conflicts in terms of a positive and historical-dialectical anthropology. As critical anthropology removes the ideological distortions of race, it can serve as a theoretical basis for the practical emancipation of oppressed races and all of humankind from the captivity of racism, maybe even of race.

3

On our planet, humankind has particularised itself into different races which correspond to divisions of the earth into continents. In these main geographical territories, races lived and evolved in relative isolation: Africans, Negroes or Blacks, Asians or Mongols; Caucasians, including Near Easterners, Europeans, Americans and Malayans. To assume (as, e.g., did Hitler)[6] that the human races are species in the zoological sense would be unscientific and utter racial ideology, for, in the case of humankind, genus and species are identical. There is only one human genus and species present on this globe. The human species which first differentiated itself along continental lines particularises itself further into racially-based nations and finally singularises itself into different racially-conditioned families and individuals, as organisms and natural subjects with different talents, temperaments, characters, life-cycles, sexuality and idiosyncrasies.

As once the human genus differentiated itself into the different races, it may very well supersede this differentiation again and return to its original identity, both preserving and elevating the non-identity of the enormous physical and spiritual enrichment contributed to history by diverse races. Racial enlightenment means to free races from fears and to make them masters of their fate in terms of a universalistic ethics. This ethics is to transcend individual, family and nation and also transcend racial in-group/out-group barriers towards global communication-without-domination (communication community) and, ultimately, God's Absolute Future.[7] Anthropological discourse as eschatological memory of racial life, suffering and death—with practical intent of racial liberation—is, of course, not easy, since anthropologists are themselves always members of a certain race or mixture of races. This difficulty can only be overcome through the anthropologist reflecting on his/her own racial dependence into his/her anthropology. Only through such reflection can critical anthropology avoid turning into ideology.

Throughout the nineteenth and twentieth centuries, philosophers as well as social and natural scientists consistently focused upon the question of mono- and poly-genesis. They thought they could, by assuming the descendence of humankind from several pairs of parents, explain the physical and spiritual superiority of one race over another. They even hoped to prove that humans are so different from each other by nature that some can rightly be dominated by others like animals. This precisely is the very core of the modern ideology of racism. It found its most terrible and cruel practical and technical application through Europeans against Africans, Asians, Middle Easterners and Native Americans and Malayans, particularly during the nineteenth and twentieth centuries. Even today, the scientific question of poly-genesis has not been conclusively decided either by physical or cultural anthropology or by theology.

Racism as the ideological doctrine of providential selection and election of human races is extremely flattering to collective egotism.[8] Racist narcissism is (like national narcissism) personal narcissism projected to the collective level, yet keener, nobler, more idealistic and more easily aroused than individual narcissism. One can commit crimes in the name of one's race which one would not dare do as an individual or would find rather obscene. In its perspectives racism has without doubt the virtue of accepting and rigorously extending, just as they occur, the lines of the tree of life. The history of the animated world does indeed show us a succession of ramifications, springing up one after the other, one on top of the other through the success and domination of a privileged group. Why should humankind be exempt from the general rule of life? Why should there not once again among the human races be valid the struggle for life and survival of the fittest, the trial of strength? The supermen should, like any other stem, be an offshoot from a single bud of mankind. The tactic of isolation of racial groups seems to be able to produce a plausible justification by pointing to the methods pursued by life for its development right down to mankind. Is there not some truth in racism?

Paradoxically, these perverse, cynical and brutal racist theories can stir a noble passion. In response, large parts of humankind can be called to violence. Racist theories, however, involve a subtle deformation of a great truth. The racists deceive themselves and others by ignoring an essential phenomenon, viz., the natural confluence of grains of thought. Racists disfigure or conceal the actual contours of the noosphere and render biologically impossible the convergence of the differentiated races and the formation of a veritable spirit of the earth, i.e., the reconciled society. Critical anthropology of race must be guided by negative dialectics, the determinate negation of untruth in powerful racist ideologies, without destruction of their truth, i.e., the racial differentiation as a genuine moment in the long march of humankind from animality to freedom.

2. THEOLOGY ALLIED TO DIALECTICAL ANTHROPOLOGY

According to philosophical anthropology from Plato and Aristotle, through Thomas Aquinas, Meister Eckhart and Nicolaus of Cues, to Kant, Hegel, Marx and Horkheimer, humankind is by nature rational: *animal rationale.*[9] Herein lies the possibility of equal human rights for all men and women of all races on all continents and the nullity of any rigid and permanent differentiation between those races having human and civil rights, e.g., Europeans, and those races not having such rights, e.g., Africans, Asians, Near Easterners, Native Americans or Malayans.

In its battle against different forms of racism based on racial differentiation and distorting it, theology can do no better than to ally itself with dialectical anthropology as it stresses the fundamental rationality, equality, freedom and human rights of all men and women in all races, on all continents, in all historical epochs. Together with dialectical anthropology, a critical political theology can liquidate the racist ontologisation of race differences and can promote their historicisation and relativisation. Since race differences came about historically, they can also disappear in a historical process.

It must be stressed that the subjective aspect must stand in the foreground in any critical investigation into racism. An investigation into the role played in the formation of racial prejudice and ideology by the object of racism can easily be excluded. The object, of course, plays a certain role, but greatest attention must be devoted to the forms of reaction directed towards the racial object rather than towards the basis of these reactions within the racial object. Actually, racist prejudice has little to do with the qualities of those members of different races against whom it is directed.

Racial prejudice is, in fact, an unconscious transfer of hostility from the masters of society, responsible for frustration and repression, onto a substitute object. In this manner, more radical manifestations of a blocking of the subject's relationship to reality is dodged. The object of this unconscious destructiveness of the racist, far from being merely a superficial scapegoat, must have certain specific characteristics. It must be tangible enough, yet not too tangible, lest it be exploded by its own realism. It must have sufficient historical backing and appear as an indisputable element of tradition. It must be defined in rigid stereotypes. Finally, the object must possess, or at least be capable of being perceived and interpreted in terms of, features which harmonise with the destructive tendencies of the racially prejudiced subject. Some of these features, such as clanishness, hypersexuality, greed, etc., aid rationalisation. Others, such as expression of weakness or masochism, provide psychologically adequate stimuli for destructiveness.

There is no doubt that all these requirements could potentially be satisfied by members of any race in a specific historical situation; any member of any race can, under certain circumstances, fulfil this function in the psychological household of many people in another race. Critical anthropology neither enumerates a diversity of psychological and sociological factors nor singles out a specific one as the cause but develops a unified framework within which all demands are united together consistently. This amounts to nothing less than a dialectical anthropology of modern society.

Racism is functional precisely by virtue of its relative independence from the racial object. Racism does not depend upon the nature of the racial object as much as upon the subject's own psychological wants and needs for, e.g., security. The racial group towards which racists direct their prejudice is incidental. American racists may concentrate their ideology simultaneously or in very fast succession against Negroes, Jews, Japanese, Arabs, etc. They blame half the evils in American society on Jews and the other half on Negroes. Racial prejudice is only superficially, if at all, related to the specific nature of the object. The relation of this to stereotype, the incapacity to have experiences, projectivity and power fantasies is only too obvious.

There is also the problem of the *cui bono*: racism as the device of the subject for effortless orientation in the cold, alienated and largely incomprehensible advanced capitalistic or socialistic society. What precisely does racism give to the subject within the concrete configurations of the adult experience? Some functions can be called rational. One need not conjure up deeper motivations to understand the attitude of the American farmer who wants to get hold of the property of his Japanese neighbour during World War II or the German businessman who wants to appropriate the property of his Jewish neighbour. One may also call rational the attitude of racists aiming at a fascist dictatorship in Nicaragua or El Salvador who accept prejudice against Native Americans as part of an overall political platform.

Ignorance and confusion prevail among racists in social matters beyond the range of their most immediate experience. The objectification of social processes and their obedience to intrinsic supra-individual laws seem to foster an intellectual alienation of the individual from society. This alienation is experienced by the individual as disorientation, with concomitant fear and uncertainty. Here the irrational imagery of the other race comes into play. The alien-ness of the racial object provides a handy formula for dealing with the alienated society. Charging the racial object with all existing evils seems to penetrate the darkness of reality like a searchlight, allowing a quick and all-encompassing orientation. Racism reduces the complexity of the world and thus brings tremendous release to the racist.

The expediency of all forms of racism (whether directed against Africans, Asians, Middle Easterners, Europeans, Native Americans or Malayans) for dominion and mastery is only too obvious. Masters use racism as distraction from economic and political problems, as cheap means of corruption, as terroristic example, while the real form of the collective and individual spirit (the prehistorical and historical entanglement into which racism is banned as desperate attempt of escape from unbearable economic and political situations) lies in complete darkness. If justice is not applied in the collective perception to suffering which is so deeply intrinsic to civilisation as racism, then the individual, too, is powerless to appease it, even if willing to do so.

Racism is inconsistent with democratic ideology. It functions as a spearhead of anti-democratic forces in organised capitalistic society, constituting pre-fascist development. The limitation of human and civil rights, consummated in the racists' idea of special treatment for racial minorities, logically implies ultimate abolition of the democratic form of government and hence, abolition of legal protection for individuals. The suggestion that a racial minority be segregated is incompatible with basic concepts of that democratic country of which the racist subject professes to be so proud. The racist metaphor of the other races being rotten apples in the barrel conjures up the imagery of evil germs, associated regularly with the dream of an effective germocide.

The metaphor of other races being cancer in the body politic expresses the racist's longing for cutting them out.

In the face of the escalating race struggle between Europeans on the one hand and Native Americans, Africans, Asians and Near Easterners on the other hand, the ability of any metaphysics is paralysed. What has happened between the races has smashed the basis of the compatibility of speculative metaphysical thought with everyday experience. What do God, freedom and immortality mean in the face of the race conflicts in America, Europe, the Middle East and Asia? Once more the dialectical motive of the turnover of quantity into quality triumphs unspeakably and ineffably. With the murder of millions of innocent victims of racism through governmental administration, death has become something never before feared in such a way. After the racial disasters of this century alone, there is no possibility that death can enter into the life experience of individuals as something compatible in any way with the normal course of life.

The recent catastrophes of this century alone have proven the failure of modern culture. That Auschwitz could happen in the midst of all tradition of philosophy and theology, art and the enlightening sciences says more than that the spirit was not able to touch people and change them. Hitler forced upon men and women in advanced capitalistic and socialistic society a new categorical imperative: viz., to direct their thinking and acting in such a way that the race struggles of the past do not repeat themselves in the future. The challenge of traditional theological words (the test if God would let this race annihilation happen without angrily interfering) is, more than the theodicy of Leibniz and Hegel, utter blasphemy.

3. VINDICATION AND RECONCILIATION

When people of a certain race are exposed to and caught up in infinite pain, which members of more powerful races give them, then they cherish and foster (like a redeeming ideal) the thought that One may come who stands in the light—the Messiah, the Christ—and who brings truth and justice to innocent victims of racial oppression. Such redemption may not occur in the lifetime of those innocent victims enslaved or gassed or lynched, but one day, racial injustice must assuredly be set right. The lies, the wrong image of the innocent victims which the members of the dominant race carry into the world and against which the murdered can no longer defend themselves, must one day fade before the truth. The real life of the victims, their thoughts, hopes and longings (just as the sufferings and injustices which were inflicted upon the oppressed race) must be revealed. It is extremely bitter for members of the oppressed race to die in darkness, being misunderstood and misjudged.

This darkness must be cleared up and lightened. It is the task and honour of historical dialectical anthropology to do this. Seldom have historicistic historians and positivistic anthropologists forgotten this task so decisively as during the efforts in this century to grant full historical 'understanding' to former dominant races and their hangman's assistants. The dream of all saints that better and more humane centuries may look upon them may have been fulfilled in such a way that present-day conservative and reactionary scholars and poets in Europe and America dream of returning into that darkness of past racial disasters. They do this not out of youthful longing to free innocent victims of racial holocausts but to present such blessed times expertly to the present generation for future use.

Past racial history carries with itself a temporal index by which it is referred to redemption. There is a secret agreement between past generations and the present one: Our coming was expected on earth. Like every generation which preceded us, we have

B

been endowed with a weak Messianic power. To this Messianic power, particularly, innocent victims of all forms of racism on all continents have a claim. As religious people as well as humanists know, that claim cannot be settled cheaply.

The Messiah comes not only as redeemer but also as subduer of the Antichrist. Only that critical anthropologist who is firmly convinced that even dead victims of race oppression will not be saved from the enemy if he wins can fan the spark of hope in the past. This enemy—racism—has not ceased to be victorious even in this decade.

The dialectical anthropologist approaches the historical problem of race as a monad, a configuration pregnant with extreme tension. In this structure the critical anthropologist recognises signs of a Messianic cessation of happening or a revolutionary chance in the fight for the oppressed races. The only anthropology which can be responsibly practised after the race catastrophes of this century and in the face of the resultant despair is that which attempts to contemplate all racial issues as they present themselves from the standpoint of redemption. Anthropological knowledge has no light but that shed on the racial holocausts by redemption; all else is merely anthropological construction and technique.

Anthropological perspectives must be fashioned which displace and estrange the world, reveal it to be (with all its contradictions of race, its racial rifts and crevices) as indignant and distorted as it will appear one day in the Messianic light. To gain such anthropological perspective without velleity or violence, entirely from felt contact with racial contradictions—this is the task of the critical anthropology of race able to overcome racism. This is the simplest of all things, because the racial situation demands such anthropological knowledge; because consummated racial negativity, once faced squarely, delineates the mirror image of its opposite, i.e., racial reconciliation. It is also an utterly impossible task, because it presupposes a standpoint removed, even slightly, from the scope of racial existence. We know very well that any possible anthropological knowledge must first of all wrest from what is the case racially, whether it shall hold good, but becomes marked for this very reason by the very race-ideological distortion and indigence from which it seeks to escape. The more passionately anthropological thought denies its racial conditionality for the sake of the unconditional—truth, redemption, Messiah—the more unconsciously and so calamitously, it is delivered up to the world of race domination. Dialectical anthropology must finally comprehend its own impossibility for the sake of the possible struggle against racism. Besides the demand this places on anthropological thought, the question of the reality or non-reality of the Messiah, the Christ and redemption is of the greatest importance.

There can be no doubt that Europeans have made great contributions to the progress of the human species on all continents, not only in terms of science, technology and economic productivity, but also in ethical and socio-ethical terms (e.g., more humane legal procedures, more rational and free constitutions, etc.). But anyone who has observed the cruel injustices which Europeans of all nations have inflicted, on all continents, upon their own race and also, particularly, on Africans, Asians, Middle Easterners, Native Americans and Malayans, can have only one mission: to co-operate with all races towards the ultimate abolition of such terrible racist behaviour and to strengthen solidarity with the innocent victims of racism who have died under unspeakable pain, torment and agony. The thinking and work of religious people and humanists of all races who have seen racism in one form or another must belong to the innocent victims. The fact that the living have escaped the racial holocaust so far must not make solidarity with victims problematic but, rather more certain. Whatever the survivors of past race struggles experience in the present or future must stand under the aspect of the racial horror which can be the sudden fate of any race.

The death of innocent victims of racism must be the truth of the life of the survivors. Survivors are here to express the desperation and longing of innocent victims of racism.

We can only hope that Europeans, in co-operation with Africans, Asians, Near Easterners, Native Americans and Malayans, will be able to produce (particularly in the American and Slavic world) a new future: a new post-European, post-modern, post-bourgeois, post-racial reconciled society of reason, freedom and peace.

Reconciliation is the highest notion of the religions of the Middle East and Europe: Judaism, Islam and Christianity; their whole meaning is the expectation of reconciliation. From the inability of dominant races to reconcile themselves with other races stems much of the paranoic reaction formation of racism. Today, once more, racists are in the process of realising the negative absolute—racial hate as the negative of racial reconciliation—out of their own power. Such hate leads to union with the racial object in its enslavement and destruction. Racists transform the world into the hell they have always perceived it as.

The metanoia in racial matters depends on the question of whether dominated races can become masters of themselves in the face of the absolute insanity of racism (e.g., apartheid in South Africa), thereby eliminating it. Only in the liberation of thought from domination and in the abolition of force and violence can the idea that each member of each race is first of all a human being realise itself. This would be the step from the racist society, which drives the dominated and the dominant race into illness, to a humane society. It would fulfil the racist lie as its own contradiction. The race question proves to be indeed the turning point of humankind's history of freedom. With the overcoming of the racist illness of the spirit, which grows exuberantly on the fertile soil of racial self-assertion unbroken by reflection and repentance, humankind turns from the general counter-race into the human genus. This human species is, as nature, nevertheless more than mere nature, as it becomes aware of its own image. The individual and social emancipation from domination is the counter-movement to the false projection of racism. No racial victim who knows how to appease this false projection in him/herself is similar to the disaster which overtakes him or her as all persecuted animals and men on this globe. Reconciliation, not hate, must be the last word of the history of race. For this reconcilation of the races, no less is required than an anthropological revolution, motivated by nothing less than a critical political theology.[10]

Notes

1. G. W. F. Hegel *System der Philosophie* (Stuttgart-Bad Cannstadt 1965) III pp. 52-254; *idem. Vorlesungen über die Äesthetik* (Frankfurt a.M. 1970) I p. 200; E. Fromm *Marx's Concept of Man* (New York 1967) VX pp. 24-43, 93-196, 197-216, 220; M. Horkheimer 'Bemerkungen zur Philosophischen Anthropologie' *Zeitschrift für Sozialforschung* (1970) IV, 1-25. (ZfS).

2. E. Kogon *Der SS Staat* (Frankfurt a.M. 1965) V-SIV pp. 46, 47, 208-232; T. W. Adorno et. al. *The Authoritarian Personality* (New York 1969) Part IV; *idem. Negative Dialektik* (Frankfurt a.M. 1966) Part III; M. Horkheimer *Zur Kritik der Instrumentellen Vernunft* (Frankfurt a.M. 1967) pp. 302-320, 335-353; W. Fach 'Reagan und die Reaktion' *Frankfurter Hefte* 36/2 (February 1981) 15-24. (FH); A. Pradetto "Systemwandel in Polen?', *FH* 36/1 (January 1981) 17-24; *FH* 36/2 (February 1981) 35-44.

3. Ch. Winick *Dictionary of Anthropology* (Peterson, New Jersey 1961) p. 448; A. Montague *Man* (New York 1961) pp. 78, 79, 180-182; T. Dobzhansky *Mankind Evolving* (New Haven 1969) chap. 10; R. Linton *The Study of Man* (New York 1964) chaps. 2, 3; R. Benedict *Patterns of Culture* (Boston 1959) pp. 9-15, 44, 233-236; B. S. Kraus *The Basis of Human Evolution* (New York 1964) pp. 204-206, 320-343, 25, 352-353; C. Kluckhohn *Mirror for Man* (New York 1949) p. 101, chap. 5; E. A. Hoebel *Man in the Primitive World* (New York 1958) Part III; W. Howells *Mankind in the*

Making (Garden City, New York 1967) chap. 18; A. L. Kroeber *Anthropology: Biology and Race* (New York) chaps, 3, 4.

4. M. Horkheimer and Th. W. Adorno *Dialektik der Aufklärung* (Frankfurt a.M. 1969) pp. 177-217.

5. A. Montague *Anthropology and Human Nature* (New York 1963) Part III; M. Horkheimer *Notizen 1950 bis 1969 und Däm-merung* (Frankfurt a.M. 1974) pp. 8, 28, 145, 157, 164, 202, 208 213; *idem.* 'Die Juden und Europa' *ZfS* VIII, 115-137; R. J. Siebert *From Critical Theory of Society to Theology of Communicative Praxis* (Washington DC 1979) chaps. 6-8.

6. A. Hitler *Mein Kampf* (Boston 1943) chap. 11.

7. *Praktiche Philosophie/Ethik* edd. K. O. Apel, D. Bohler et. al. (Frankfurt a.M. 1980) chaps. 1, 4, 6, 7; R. J. Siebert 'Communication Without Domination' *Concilium* 111 (1978) 81-94.

8. Teilhard de Chardin *The Phenomenon of Man* (New York 1965) p. 238.

9. G. W. F. Hegel *Vorlesungen über die Geschichte der Philosophie* (Frankfurt a.M. 1971) II pp. 105-132, 198-221, 564-565; III pp. 329-386.

10. G. W. F. Hegel *Vorlesungen über die Philosophie des Rechts* (Stuttart-Bad Cannstadt 1965) pp. 19-36; J. B. Metz *Jenseits bürgerlicher Religion* (München 1980) chaps. 2 and 3.

Alan Davies

The Ideology of Racism

ACCORDING TO Hannah Arendt, an ideology is simply the logic of an idea which takes history as its subject matter and interprets events as the unfolding of its own inherent laws.[1] Life, in other words, is squeezed into the idea, and made to conform to its dictates. In this sense, ideologies are recent in time, being creations of the nineteenth century when certain ideas were absolutised in western thought.

1. THE MYTH OF RACIAL SUPERIORITY

The idea of race as the key to history was suggested in Britain by Robert Knox (*Races of Man*, 1850) and in France by Arthur de Gobineau (*Essai sur l'inégalité des races humaines*, 1853-55). From the former arose the myth of Saxon—later Anglo-Saxon—racial genius and from the latter arose the myth of Aryan racial genius; both myths, however, were variants on the general theme of white European superiority over coloured non-Europeans. Their genesis was political. Knox sought to prove that Saxon man was 'nature's democrat' and therefore the future ruler of the earth. Gobineau, on the other hand, disliked democracy and sought to prove that its rise was a sure sign of the decay and impending death of civilisation. In either case, the non-white races were relegated to an inferior status as symbols of the primitive and uncreative elements in human nature. They were either incapable of democracy or responsible for it.

Both the optimism of Knox and the pessimism of Gobineau were conceived in the same psychological and social womb: alienation. Knox despised Victorian Britain with its (in his view) undemocratic political system. An ardent republican, he regarded the British monarchy as fit only for 'dynasty-loving Celts' and antagonistic to the true English, i.e., Saxon race. Everywhere, Saxons were smashing the shackles of tyranny and someday, he predicted, on American soil would arise a mighty 'republican empire' as the apotheosis of nature's democrat—Saxon man.[2] Thus would the Saxon avenge himself on the Celt! Gobineau despised republican France with its democratic political system. A nostalgic conservative, he ragarded the 'Gallic' bourgeoisie as unfit rulers and Paris as a racial cesspool filled with violent riffraff ready to tear down everything noble and beautiful in French culture. Alienated from his own society, he transferred the supposed commercial instincts of the middle class onto Orientals and the supposed bestiality of the lower class onto Blacks, reserving the supposed aristocratic qualities of the upper class for the white race.[3] His Aryan, consequently, was merely an idealised

11

self-portrait: the kind of man Gobineau imagined himself to be. Despite their differences, the Anglo-Saxon and Aryan race myths were fabrications of the western psyche fixated on itself during the radical changes, impossible dreams and profound insecurities of the modern age. The proper term for such self-infatuation is narcissism.

Both myths were inspired by a hoary theme, derived from Tacitus (*Germania*, 98), that the Germanic tribes of antiquity were the unspoiled children of nature: virile, courageous and freedom-loving. These attributes were transmitted to Britain by Hengest and Horsa and to France by the Frankish (German) conquerors of old Gaul; thus they supplied the racial foundations of both nations. Later, when the theory of an original white (Aryan) race in central Asia became popular as a result of linguistic discoveries linking the European, Persian and Sanskrit languages, the German connection acquired a new significance. For the pre-Christian Teuton was also an Aryan, a descendant of one of those 'columns of masterful men' who had once marched down 'from the roof of the world'.[4] With this historic fusion, the Aryan-Teutonic-Frankish-Saxon bearer of the torch of civilisation supplied an irresistible racial simile whereby the Europeans could exalt themselves above others. It also provided a religious myth whereby the alienated European could recover his lost spiritual vitality through rediscovering his 'primordial Ancestor'—that 'exemplary model that must be imitated in order to recover racial "purity", physical strength, nobility, (and) the heroic "ethics" of the glorious and creative "beginnings" '.[5] This sense of reinvigoration was the secret of the tremendous dynamism of the racist ideology in the modern world.

By definition, a race myth requires inferior races and moves in a dualistic direction as time proceeds. When the racists concentrated their gaze *outside* of Europe, denigration of Orientals and Blacks was paramount (the older Gobineau became obsessed with the 'yellow peril'). When racist eyes were focused *inside* Europe, where few Orientals or Blacks were found, the silhouette of the Semite loomed large. Gobineau was not especially anti-Semitic. Semites (Jews) were debased Aryans through the infusion of Black blood, but the lowest kind of white man was higher than the highest kind of yellow or Black man. However, with the need to define an enemy, a type of 'racial Manichaeism'[6] soon developed. If the Aryan was the idealised European, the Semite became the demonised (half-Black?) non-European: the alien intruder responsible for the ills of the age. Among the later Gobinists, Aryan and Semite became counter-symbols of beauty and ugliness, creative and destructive, good and evil power locked in a social struggle for control of Europe. While *Jews* were real enough, *Semites* were clearly invented, but this fiction did not matter. In racism, fictional races are just as important as real races.

2. SCIENTIFIC JUSTIFICATIONS

Living, as we now do, after the mass destruction of the European Jews at Nazi hands, we are acutely aware of the dangers of racist ideology in all its forms. In the nineteenth century, however, race ideas were usually not seen in a sinister light. For one thing, Darwinism—at its peak towards the end of the century—endowed these ideas with a scientific aura through such concepts as natural selection. To the Social Darwinists who arose in Darwin's wake, the natural right of the higher species to prevail over the lower was indisputable. Anglo-Saxon supremacists as well as continental anti-Semites accepted the axiom that the highest race was entitled to the greatest living space, even if the living space of others had to be violated. This right could not be realised without a contest of strength, but does not biology teach us that struggle is the essence of life? One advantage of taking nature as the textbook of history is that its lessons are seldom hard to read. Darwin's cousin, Sir Francis Galton, founded the science of eugenics in order to breed better Englishmen for the sake of the empire. Was it not 'monstrous', he argued, that 'the races best fitted to play their part on the stage of life' should be 'crowded out by the incompetent, the ailing and the desponding?'[7] Galton never anticipated the Nazis with their terrible Aryan child-farms and their calculated murder of the unfit, but the 'responsible society' that Hitler established owed more than a little to Galton's ideas as passed on through German admirers.

The Social Darwinist apostles of Anglo-Saxondom could afford to think optimistically about the future because their biological interpretations of society were infused with older Enlightenment assumptions. Evolution was equated with progress and human perfectibility. Thus a roseate glow surrounded their vision of the twentieth century, when Anglo-Saxon man will have spread his limbs over the entire globe, striding the hemispheres 'from the rising to the setting sun'[8] and making many new 'English' nations after his likeness. 'Chili (sic), La Plata, and Peru must eventually become English; the Red Indian race . . . cannot stand against our colonists, and the future of the table-lands of Africa and that of Japan and of China is as clear.'[9] While Social Darwinism could produce pacifism and cosmopolitanism as well as imperialism (e.g., Herbert Spencer), it usually encouraged the latter. In spite of the *Pax Britannica*, or perhaps because of it, the nineteenth century managed to glorify war to a degree that only terrorist fanatics would approve today. War, John Ruskin declared (*The Crown of Wild Olive*, III, 93), 'is the foundation of all the arts . . . of all the high virtues and faculties of men'. War invigorates a nation, stimulates its heroism and elevating its spirit. It is also the means of social evolution, accomplishing in the external domain the same racial purpose that eugenics accomplishes in the internal domain. A thoroughbred people, like thoroughbred dogs, will prevail in any contest.

With these guidelines in mind, a generation of physical anthropologists devoted themselves to sorting out the various racial strains in Europe and elsewhere. Typically, they concentrated on skull shapes on the premise that a long head denotes a better intelligence and a more noble spirit than a broad head. Georges Vacher de Lapouge (*Les sélections sociales*, 1896) ingeniously divided the Europeans into three racial types: 'European man' (the true Aryan), 'Alpine man' and 'Mediterranean man'. A disciple of both Gobineau and Darwin, Lapouge also represented the disaffected part of French society that hated the revolutionary legacy in French politics, since the revolution had committed the racial sin of executing the 'eugenic' aristocrats. Such acts were against nature and its biological laws. Should long heads disappear in the racial composition of the West, civilisation was probably doomed. Unfortunately for the anthropologists, however, no real agreement was ever reached concerning the exact criteria of race and racial differentiation. What their statistics based on cephalic measurements really proved was the ease whereby ideas accepted on quite unscientific grounds could be covered with a scientific mantle. Of course, as Paul Tillich knew,[10] myth in the modern world has to present itself in scientific guise in order to be believed.

In this fashion, a new ethic grounded in a new natural law became the basis of a new ideology that at once regarded itself as the true science, the true philosophy and the true religion. Like all authentic world views, racism supplied a point of departure for thinking in general, deciphering the mystery of human existence through its own cosmic lens. The racist universe was essentially materialistic. Only nature, according to the racist philosopher H. S. Chamberlain (*The Foundations of the Nineteenth Century*, 1899), is truly free; human freedom lies in subservience to nature's laws. Transcendence in its old biblical and theological sense does not exist, nor could the genuine racist accept the concept of a Creator. Such biblical doctrines merely produced a religion of fear and attitudes of 'submissive and slavish' obedience[11]—in other words, Semitic religion. Aryan religion, on the other hand, is rooted in a courageous affirmation of 'merciless fate';[12] like the ancient Stoics, the Aryan dies in a dignified and joyful manner, embracing but also defying his own destruction. Jesus was not a Semite but an Aryan. According to the American racist Madison Grant,[13] Christ, the greatest member of the 'great race', was blond and Nordic like the Olympian gods; suggestively, he was crucified between two 'brunet' thieves! To the French racists, Christ was a Jupiter figure, or type of Latin god.[14] Nothing could better illustrate the religious positivism of the racist mind than these narcissistic distortions of Christianity.

Obviously, the rejection of transcendence was part of the general trend towards secularism of the modern age. In this respect, the racists were not unique. Michael Biddiss points out that the secular notions of race and class (as well as nation) arose out of the fragments of the old Christian cosmos, for only its fragmentation allowed Gobineau to isolate the concept of race as it had allowed Karl Marx to isolate the concept of class.[15] Hence racism and Marxism became secular religions for many of their followers. It is interesting that the nineteenth-century racists like the nineteenth-century socialists were often alienated from the capitalistic industrial order, especially on the continent, and that it was possible to be both a racist and a socialist at once. In France, Gustave Tridon and Albert Regnard—both Communards and disciples of the anarchist Auguste Blanqui—distinguished Aryan socialism and Semitic capitalism, as did Edmond Picard in Belgium. These political radicals believed that only Aryans were capable of 'social renovation' in a decadent period.[16] Despite these examples, however, racism usually developed into an ideology of the right rather than the left. This is because the racists usually turned to the past (e.g., tribal origins) and the socialists to the future for their visions of an alternate society. At once similar and different, racism and Marxism became the two great competing 'isms' of the twentieth century during the crisis of the West.

3. ROOTS IN THE PAST

While ra*cism* in its ideological sense was the product of the nineteenth century, its antecedents in race-thinking stretch back to antiquity. Ethnocentrism, or the tendency of every tribe to identify humankind only with its own members, is ancient in time and always has racial overtones. One finds this tendency even in great civilisations with universal pretensions. Aristotle, for example, thought that the barbarians were 'natural slaves' (*Politics*, I, vi) and the Hellenistic Greeks regarded themselves as the privileged donors of enlightenment to the lesser breeds without the law. Graeco-Roman culture, while mostly free of colour prejudice, nevertheless in Christian times employed the visual metaphors of whiteness and blackness to denote goodness and evil. Did not Christ come into the world to make the souls if not the bodies of Blacks inwardly *white*? Christian civilisation, moreover, despite its quasi-universalism, inherited the Graeco-Roman sense of ethnic superiority. During the middle ages, a white Christendom imagined itself encircled by menacing pagan realms both literally and figuratively darker: the 'children of light' surrounded by the 'children of darkness'! In one sense, colonial expansion at the end of the medieval period was a kind of final crusade against the children of darkness—an outburst of the European 'cultural, racial, political and social "superiority-complex" '.[17]

When Europeans encountered unfamiliar peoples in great numbers on remote continents during this final crusade, racial speculation was stimulated enormously. The different types of human beings seemed too different to be reduced to a common denominator. Hence, the biblical account of a single human origin (monogenesis) was slowly replaced by theories of multiple origin (polygenesis), and the various races were graded on a scale with, of course, the white European (who did the grading) at the top. Whiteness itself was assumed to be the normative human condition; darker skin colours were therefore the result of either sickness or degeneracy—deviations from the norm. Depending on the bias of the observer, this view could be justified on scientific (physical environment?) or on religious grounds (the biblical myth of Ham, *Gen.* 9:20-27). According to an old rabbinic exegesis, God's curse on the descendants of Ham took the form of blackening their skins (*Babylonian Talmud*, Sanhedrin II). Christian interpreters eventually copied this idea. In any case, by the end of the eighteenth century, few Europeans were not in one form or another persuaded of their own racial supremacy. Even the Age of Reason was flawed with the same ethnocentric pride as an older Christendom and a still older classical civilisation, as David Hume demonstrates:

> I am apt to suspect the negroes and in general all the other species of men . . . to be naturally inferior to the whites. There never was a civilized nation of any other complexion than white, nor even any individual eminent either in action or speculation. No ingenious manufacturers amongst them, no arts, no sciences. On the other hand, the most rude and barbarous of the whites, such as the ancient GERMANS, the present TARTARS, have still something eminent about them, in their valour, form of government, or some other particular. Such a uniform and constant difference could not happen in so many countries and ages, if nature had not made an original distinction betwixt these breeds of men.

With such opinions, European race-thinking was already trembling on the verge of racism. The portents were clear, and the latter only awaited the Aryan myth and the mood of the nineteenth century.

4. CONCLUSION

After Auschwitz, the Aryan myth sank into odium with its moral aura terribly tarnished. Never again—in my opinion—is it likely to be believed by large numbers of people, although its ghost lingers on and attempts at a resurrection still occur. Anglo-Saxondom, as the myth of Germany's victors in 1945, did not perish so suddenly; however, it has suffered a slow demise as a result of post-war British decline and America's weakening hegemony. Indeed, all pre-war myths of white supremacy (e.g., Afrikanerdom), where they still exist today, seem more as defence mechanisms against the winds of change than as triumphalistic visions of a soon-to-be-realised future. But their demise does *not* mean that racism itself is dead. On the contrary, the rebirth of racism is one of the most ominous signs of our era. Racism, like a Hindu god, may have many incarnations. Precisely because the ideology is no longer respectable, racist views today possess an incognito character, incarnating themselves in systems of social, political and economic power, concealing themselves behind bland bureaucratic façades. This is not so much ideological as 'structural' racism: a racism that need not identify itself as racist, but which can exercise great demonic energy in the world. It is mostly this form of racism that confronts us today. To struggle against it is far harder than to struggle against the unenlightened minds of old-fashioned racists who remember Gobineau, Knox, Chamberlain and Lapouge.

Notes

1. H. Arendt *The Origins of Totalitarianism* (New York 1964) p. 469.
2. R. Knox *Races of Men* (London 1862) p. 11.
3. See G. L. Mosse *Toward the Final Solution* (New York 1980) p. 53.

4. L. Poliakov *The Aryan Myth* trans. Edmund Howard (London 1974) p. 191.

5. M. Eliade *Myth and Reality* trans. Willard R. Trask (New York 1963) p. 183.

6. Poliakov in the work cited in note 4, p. 272.

7. F. Galton *Hereditary Genius* (Gloucester, Mass. 1972) p. 27.

8. J. Fiske *American Political Ideas* (New York 1885) p. 143.

9. C. W. Dilke *Greater Britain* (Philadelphia 1869) p. 105.

10. P. Tillich *The Socialist Decision* trans. Franklin Sherman (New York 1977) p. 41.

11. H. F. K. Günther *The Religious Attitudes of the Indo-Europeans* trans. Vivian Bird (London 1967) p. 24.

12. *Ibid.* p. 30.

13. M. Grant *The Passing of the Great Race* (New York 1923) p. 230.

14. See W. C. Buthman *The Rise of Integral Nationalism in France* (New York 1970) p. 152.

15. M. D. Biddiss *Father of Racist Ideology* (London 1970) p. 104.

16. See E. Silberner 'French Socialism and the Jewish Question 1865-1914' *Historia Judaica* XVI (April 1954) 6f.

17. A. Th. Van Leeuwen *Christianity in World History* trans. H. H. Hoskins (New York 1964) pp. 264-265.

Cain Felder

Racial Ambiguities in the Biblical Narratives

THE QUESTIONS of race and racism in the biblical corpus are thorny issues lodged in a dense thicket of ethnographic, philological, theological and historical complexities if not controversies. The specific racial type of the Hebrews is itself quite difficult to determine with any precision.[1] Indeed, it has come to be generally recognised that they most probably emerge as an amalgamation of races rather than from any pure racial stock. To refer to the earliest Hebrews as 'Semites' does not take us very far, inasmuch as this eighteenth-century term designates no race but a language group, embracing Hebrew, Akkadian, Arabic as well as Ethiopic (Ge'ez).[2] Thus, the language of 'burnt-face' Africans finds itself equally as Semitic as the language of the Jews and Arabs.[3] In terms of race, therefore, the Bible offers no discrete notion or explicit systematic development; rather from beginning to end, it confronts us with certain fundamental ambiguities.

In the brief compass of this article, we will examine some of the ambivalence which surfaces in the Bible as it hints at the problem of race and opens itself possibly to the charge of ethnocentrism if not incipient racism. We propose to suggest a few lines along which future discussions on the subject might take place in a more productive way for scholarly inquiry. The thesis to be examined here is that in the biblical corpus two broad processes, related to racism, may be operating. First, there is the phenomenon of 'sacralisation' by which we mean the transposing of an ideological concept into a tenet of religious faith in order to serve the vested interest of a particular ethnic group. Second, is the process of 'secularisation' or the diluting of a rich religious concept under the weighty influence of secular pressures (social or political).[4] In this second process ideas are wrenched from their original religious moorings in such a way as to fall prey to nationalistic ideologies. These often cultivate patterns of ethnocentrism and even racism which in turn can have harmful effects on certain racial groups who are inevitably scorned and marginalised.

1. RACE AND SACRALISATION IN THE OLD TESTAMENT

One of the most poignant instances of 'sacralisation' confronts us quite early in the Old Testament within the genealogies of the so-called descendants of Noah. It is

17

especially important to consider the so-called Table of Nations (Genesis 10) with the genealogy listing of I Chronicles 1:1-2:1ff. On the one hand, these listings purport to be comprehensive catalogues and have all too often been erroneously taken to be reliable sources of ancient ethnography. On the other hand, critical study of these genealogies illuminates the clear theological motives which inevitably yield an increasing tendency to prioritise the importance of the Israelites as a more important ethnic and national entity than all other peoples of the earth. We shall first examine the deceptive quality of these Old Testament genealogies and then show how their evident 'sacralisation' parallels yet another instance of 'sacralisation', namely, the whole notion of election (chosen people).

While at first glance, Gen. 10 has the appearance of being a single listing of ancient nations, biblical criticism has for some time demonstrated that Gen. 10 represents a conflation of at least two different lists, i.e., Jahwist (J) and Priestly (P) separated by centuries.[5] In fact, the conflation of different traditions in Gen. 10 doubtlessly accounts for such discrepancies as determining the land of Cush, the differences between Seba and Sheba, or the relationship between Cush and Sheba. For example, Gen. 10:7 mentions Seba (ṣeb'a) as a son of Cush, whereas Sheba (šeb'a) is the grandson of Cush according to Gen. 10:8. Here the text is clearly identifying the descendants of Ham (ḥ'am). Then in Gen. 10:28, the text introduces an anomaly, since Sheba (šeb'a) is at this point mentioned as a direct descendant not of Ham but of Shem. Furthermore, since the initial Samech of ṣeb'a is the equivalent of and interchangeable with the Hebrew Shin in Old South Arabic,[6] one could argue that Gen. 10 offers us two persons named Sheba as descendants of Cush, but only one person by that name as a descendant of Shem. In any case, it is clear that the Table of Nations as it stands does not at all have the motive of delineating sharp ethnic differences between the ancient peoples of Africa, South Arabia and Mesopotamia. The true motive lies elsewhere.

Rather than any objective historical account of genealogies, the Table of Nations in Gen. 10 presents us with a theologically motivated catalogue of people. The Table not only ends with the descendants of Shem, but does so in a way consciously stylised to accentuate the importance of the descendants of Shem among the peoples of the earth.[7] About this, the author of the genealogy in I Chron. 1:17-34 is most explicit, inasmuch as of all the descendants of the sons of Noah those descended from Shem receive the most elaborate attention. Thus, to the most primitive J listing of the nations, Gen. 10 is centuries later theologically edited according to the post-exilic Priestly tradition in order to prioritise the descendants of Shem only to be followed by a further elaboration, again centuries later, found in the genealogies of I Chronicles. In this long progression, the theological presuppositions of a particular ethnic group displace any concern for objective historiography and ethnography. The descendants of Noah apart from those of Shem are increasingly insignificant and gain access to the text only as they serve as foils to demonstrate the priority of the Israelites.

The subtle process being described may consequently be called 'sacralisation' because it represents an attempt on the part of succeeding generations of one ethnic group to construe salvation history in terms distinctly favourable to it as opposed to others. Here, ethnic particularity evolves with a certain divine vindication and inevitably the dangers of rank racism lie just beneath the surface. In fact, Num. 12 attests all too well to the manner in which individuals can so quickly move from a sacred ethnic particularity to racism of the worst sort.

In Num. 12:1, Moses' brother and sister castigate him for having married a Cushite woman (hā'išah hacūšîth). Several factors point to the probability that the offensive aspect of the marriage was the woman's black identity. In the first place, this is clearly the view expressed in the wording of the LXX ἕνεκεν τῆς γυναικὸς τῆς Αἰθιοπίσσης ('on account of the Ethiopian woman').[8] Secondly, in the rather oddly selective punishment which God unleashes upon Miriam (v. 9), it can hardly be accidental that the affliction of leprosy is described vividly 'leprous, as white as snow'. Quite an intentional contrast is dramatised here, i.e., Moses' black wife accursed by Miriam and Aaron is now contrasted with Miriam who suddenly becomes 'as white as snow' in her punishment. The contrast is sharpened all the more, since only Miriam is punished for an offence in which Aaron is equally guilty. The LXX witness together with these exegetical considerations point strongly to the probability that more than arrogance is at issue in this text. Also involved is a rebuke to the racial prejudice characterised by the attitudes of Miriam and Aaron.

That God in the Numbers 12 narrative sternly rebukes the blatant racial prejudice of Miriam and Aaron is a perennial reminder of the extraordinary progressive racial values of the Bible in comparison to medieval and modern hostile racial attitudes.[9] At the same time, however, the Numbers 12 narrative exposes further the inherent difficulties with any quick generality about the racial implications of the process of 'sacralisation' which surfaces when early traditions assume, through years of refinement, an ethnic particularity which circumstantially marginalises other groups which stand outside of the Torah, 'ereṣ Iśraēl, and the Covenant.

Largely for theological reasons, the process of 'sacralisation' in the Old Testament remains racially ambiguous especially with specific reference to Black people. The distinction which the Old Testament makes is not racial, but between a divinely justified ethnic or national entity and all who do not belong to or identify with the terms of salvation outlined in the criteria of the 'in-group'. It is therefore surprising to many that Black people are not only frequently mentioned in numerous Old Testament texts but are also mentioned in ways that are most favourable in terms of acknowledging their actual and potential role in the salvation history of Israel. By no means are Black people excluded from the particularity of Israel's story as long as they claim it, however secondarily, and not proclaim their own story apart from the activity of Israel's God.

Extensive lists of Old Testament passages which make favourable reference to Black people are readily accessible.[10] Let a few illustrations of these provocative texts suffice. Isa. 37:9 and II Kings 19:9 refer to Tirharka, King of the Ethiopians, who was actually the third member of the Twenty-fifth Egyptian Dynasty which ruled all of Egypt (689-664 BC).[11] According to the biblical texts, Tirharka was the object of the desperate hopes of Israel; it was he who, in the days of Hezekiah, was seen as possibly intervening with his armies to stave off the impending Assyrian assault of Sennacherib. More than a half century later, another text could refer to 'the mighty men of Ethiopia and Punt who handle the shield' (Jer. 46:9). Indeed the Old Testament indicates that Black people were part of the Hebrew army (II Sam. 18:21-32) and even part of the royal court and the 'Ebĕd-mĕlek not only intervening to save Jeremiah's life (Jer. 38:7-13) but also the object of a singular divine blessing (Jer. 39:15-18). The dominant portrait of the Ethiopians in the Old Testament is that of a wealthy people (Job 28:19; Isa. 45:14) who would soon experience conversion (Ps. 68:31; Isa. 11:11, 18:7; Zeph. 3:10).

This sympathetic and racially positive Old Testament portrait of the Ethiopians, of course, has another side. The nations of Africa, as was the case with all nations in the Hebrew view, were subject to divine wrath and judgment (Ezek. 30:1-5, Isa. 20:3, Zeph. 2:12). This attitude reveals the subtle process of 'sacralisation' in the Old Testament quite clearly. In the Old Testament, Black people ultimately gain significance only as they affirm and identify with the central tenets of Israel's faithstory; apart from this they are marginal with no independent story of their own. From the reckoning of the Table of Nations to the varied prophetic oracles, this basic fact serves as the 'Catch 22' of the Old Testament writers. The result is a strong theological justification for the pre-eminence of one ethnic group in the order of creation which is inescapably dangerous for any ethnic or racial entity.

2. ELECTION AND SACRALISATION IN THE BIBLE

Israel's particularity as considered in the foregoing discussion of race and 'sacralisation' loses much of its subtlety as the dubious concept of her election (*bāḥār*) begins to gain a firm footing in the Old Testament. Certainly, although traces of the idea of Israel's chosenness and personal special relationship with her deity were present in 'the pre-Jahwistic cult of the ancestors', the explicit concept of Jahweh's loving preference for the people of Israel develops relatively late.[12] The theologically elaborated belief that Jahweh specifically chose Israel above all other nations does not become a matter of religious ideology and hence an instance of 'sacralisation' until the period of Deuteronomistic history towards the end of the seventh century (Deut. 7:6-8; 10:15; Jer. 2:3, cf. Isa. 43:20; 65:9).[13]

Regardless of the theological structure which attempts to support the Deuteronomistic concept of Israel's election, ambiguities almost immediately engulf this concept of election. Horst Seebass, for example, insists that even among the Deuteronomistic writers, Israel's election 'only rarely stands at the centre of what is meant by *electio*'.[14] According to him, *bāḥār* as a technical term for Israel's election always functions as a symbol of universalism, i.e., represents Israel in the role of 'service to the whole'.[15] Seebass is representative of those who want to de-emphasise the distinctive ethnic or racial significance of the concept in Israel's self-understanding in the Deuteronomistic period.[16]

The ethnic and racial ambiguities involved in the concept of Israel's election seem to persist, albeit with many rationales to the contrary. The ambiguity does not so much result from the fact that a universalistic history is presupposed by the biblical writers who advance the Old Testament concept of Israel's election; rather the ambiguities stem from the nature of the universalism which is presupposed. G. von Rad points out that in the Deuteronomistic circles, the chosenness of Israel attains a radical form and its universal aspect is at best paradoxical.[17] One might further suggest that perhaps on one level the paradox resides in the notion that Israel's election in a universal divine scheme seems to lead inevitably to 'sacralisation' with the people of Israel as an ethnic group at the centre. Certainly, the Deuteronomistic authors struggled to demonstrate Jahweh's singular affirmation of the Davidic monarchy and, more importantly, Jahweh's selection of Jerusalem as the centre of any continuing redemptive activity.[18] Again, it seems quite paradoxical that, although the people of Israel exhibit no extraordinary attributes or values by which they objectively merit Jahweh's election, there develops particularly in post-exilic Judaism an elaborate doctrine of merit by which those who know and follow the Torah within Israel as an ethnic group attempt to prove their worthiness as the chosen people.

Despite the absence of any inherent superiority of the people of Israel in their lengthy biblical documentary of their own sin and instances of faithlessness, the concept of election becomes inextricably bound up with ethnic particularity. Accordingly, the people of Israel arrogate to themselves the status of being pre-eminently chosen and thereby claim to possess the Law, Covenant, a continuing promise of the Land and the City as the 'in-group'. At the same time, all who stand outside the community or apart from the supporting religious ideology of election are relegated to the margins of Israel's 'universal' saving history. In this progression, as we have seen, other races and ethnic groups may, of course, subscribe to Israel's religious ideology and derive the commensurate benefits, but always the criteria for such subscription seem to be mediated through the predilections of an ethnic group reinforced by elaborate genealogies and the transmission of particular legal religious traditions.

This entire development typifies what we have called the process of 'sacralisation' and it is striking indeed to see the very different way by which election comes to be treated in the New Testament. George Foot Moore provides us with a glimpse of the different conception which one encounters in the New Testament, when he asserts that, for the Old Testament idea of national election, 'Paul and the Church substituted an individual election to eternal life, without regard to race or station'.[19] Such an assertion, however, grossly oversimplifies New Testament ideas about election. Rudolf Bultmann provides us with a more helpful understanding of the New Testament in this regard. He argues that in the New Testament 'the Christian Church becomes the true people of God'; in Bultmann's view, the New Testament no longer concerns itself with a pre-eminent ethnic group, i.e., Ἰσραὴλ κατὰ σάρκα (I Cor. 10:18), but with the Israel of God (Gal. 6:16) without any exclusive ethnic co-ordinates.[20]

In contrast to the Deuteronomistic usage of bāḥār, the New Testament never presents the term ἐκλέγομαι or its nominal derivative ἐκλεκτός ('chosen') and ἐκλογη ('election') in an ethnically restrictive or exclusive sense. Paul wants to maintain a certain continuity with aspects of Israel's election in the Old Testament, but that continuity is neither ethnic nor cultic (Rom. 9:11; 11:2, 11, 28-29). For Paul, corporate election can include some Jews, but it must also embrace gentiles (Rom. 11:25; Gal. 3:28); being 'in' and 'with' Christ becomes the new crux interpretum. In Paul's view, God chose (ἐξελέξατο) the foolish, weak and low (I Cor. 1:27-28). For James, God chose (ἐξελεξατο) the poor who are rich in faith; for Matthew, God calls many, but chooses only the few (Matt. 22:14). The new universalism and unity to be found in the Christian Church expresses itself further within the context of 'God's chosen ones' in the consciously new sequence of thoughts found in Col. 3:11-12).

The only New Testament text which refers to Christians as a chosen race (γένος ἐκλεκτόν) is I Peter 2:9. Yet, in the text of I Peter, this phrase is manifestly metaphorical. I Peter 2:9 depends very heavily on the wording found in (LXX) Isa. 43:20-21, but the ethnic particularity implied in the Old Testament text has fallen away entirely in I Peter.[21] Thus, by the end of the first century, and throughout the New Testament period which extends into the second century the elect in Christian literature becomes virtually synonymous with the Church and more particularly those true believers within the confines of the Church in the world, without any explicit ethnic or racial restrictions.[22]

3. SECULARISATION IN THE NEW TESTAMENT

Ambiguities with regard to race in the New Testament do not appear within the context of what we have defined as 'sacralisation'. Accordingly, we have tried to show that especially in terms of an ethnically focused idea of corporate election or 'Israel according to the flesh' the New Testament is disapproving. In fact, the New Testament offers no grand genealogies designed to sacralise the myth of any inherent and divinely sanctioned superiority of Greeks and Romans in any manner comparable to the Table of Nations found in Gen. 10. Consequently, if one is to explore the subject of racialist tendencies in the New Testament narratives, one must turn to a different phenomenon, namely, the process of 'secularisation'. The question now becomes, How did the expanding Church, in her attempt to survive without the temporary protection she derived by being confused with Judaism, begin to succumb to the dominant symbols and ideologies of the Graeco-Roman world? We will want to see how, in this development, the universalism of the New Testament diminishes as Athens and Rome become substituted for Jerusalem of the Old Testament, as, in effect, the new centres for God's redemptive activity.

The conceptualisation of the world by early Christian authors in New Testament times, scarcely included Africa and did not at all include the Americas or the Far East.

These early Christian writers referred to Spain as 'the limits of the West'; they envisioned the perimeters of the world as the outer reaches of the Roman Empire.[23] For New Testament authors, Roman socio-political realities as well as the language and culture of Hellenism often arbitrated the ways in which God was seen as acting in Jesus Christ. Just as Jerusalem in the Old Testament had come to represent Jahweh's central city, Rome as the ultimate destination of the Christian kerygma became the new focus of the Christian missionary movement.[24]

It is no coincidence that Mark, the earliest composer of a Passion Narrative, goes to such great lengths to show that the confession of the Roman centurion (only here the Latinism κεντυρίων [centurio] in the synoptic parallel passages) brings his whole gospel narrative to its climax.[25] For his part, Luke expends considerable effort to specify the positive qualities of his various centurions (ἑκατοντάρχης).[26] There is even a sense in which they represent Rome as the capital of the gentile world, for their incipient acts of faith or confessions, according to Luke, find their dénouement in the Acts 28 portrait of the kerygma being preached in Rome. The immediate significance of this New Testament tendency to focus upon Rome instead of Jerusalem is that the darker races outside the Roman orbit are circumstantially marginalised by New Testament authors.

For lack of more descriptive terminology, this process by which the darker races are marginalised in the New Testament may be called 'secularisation'. Here, socio-political realities of the secular framework tend to dilute the New Testament vision of racial inclusiveness and universalism. Early traditions accordingly are adapted at later stages in such a way as both to expose an undue compromising of a religious vision and to show how secular socio-political realities cause religious texts to be slanted to the detriment of the darker races. Perhaps one of the most cogent illustrations of this process of 'secularisation' is Luke's narrative about the baptism and conversion of the Ethiopian official in Acts 8:26-40.

On the surface, Acts 8:26-40 is a highly problematic text. One wonders immediately if the Ethiopian finance minister of the κανδάκη, i.e., the Queen of Meroë, is a Jew or gentile. One also wonders about the efficacy of his baptism and whether it constituted or led to a full conversion to Christianity. Probably the best survey of the several problems posed by this pericope is that by Ernst Haenchen who entitles the pericope 'Philip Converts a Chamberlain'.[27] According to Haenchen, Luke is intentionally ambiguous about the Ethiopian's identity as a gentile or Jew, since Luke merely appeals to this conversion story in order to suggest 'that with this new convert the mission has taken a step beyond the conversion of Jews and Samaritans'.[28] The story itself derives from Hellenistic circles and represents for Luke, in Haenchen's view, a parallel and rival to Luke's own account of Cornelius as the first gentile-convert under the auspices of Peter.[29] Haenchen detects no particularly significant racial difficulties posed by Acts 8:26-40. For him, Luke merely edits this Hellenistic tradition to conform to his own theological design.

While we today certainly need to be reminded that in Hellenistic Christian circles of the first century it was believed that a Nubian was the first gentile-convert, Luke's awkward use of this story seems to have certain racial implications which cannot be ignored. In an attempt to address some of these racial implications, we by no means want to suggest that Luke had a negative attitude about Black people. On the contrary, one need only consider the list of the Antiochene church leadership which Luke presents in Acts 13:1 to dispel such notions. There Luke mentions one 'Symeon who is called the black man' (Συμεὼν ὁ καλούμενος Νίγερ). The Latinism here probably reinforces the idea that this Symeon was a dark-skinned person, possibly an African. Furthermore, we hasten to add that in no way do we think it important or useful to attempt to show, on the basis of any of the traditions in Acts of the Apostles, that the first gentile-convert was a Nubian as opposed to an Italian. This would be, of course, absurd, given the confessional nature of Luke's second volume which does not come to us as objective history. The racial implications of Luke's theological design are important, however, because Luke's editorialising results in a de-emphasis of a Nubian (African) in favour of an Italian (European) and enables thereby Europeans to claim that the text of Acts demonstrates some divine preference for Europeans.

In all of this, Luke himself is not innocent. His apologetics to Roman officials as well as the great significance which he attaches to Rome as the centre of the world betrays the subtle way in which Luke's theology fell prey to secular ideological ideas.[30] In the last third of the first century, the Church generally struggled to survive in an increasingly hostile political environment. Luke, not unlike other New Testament writers of this period and after,[31] seeks to assuage the wrath of Rome by allowing his theological framework to be determined by the assumption of a Roman-centred world. In this process of 'secularisation' darker races of the world are circumstantially marginalised and the New Testament vision of universalism becomes little more than rhetoric in the hands of a Euro-centric church.

'Secularisation' in the New Testament is a process which needs much fuller exploration in terms of its racial dimensions. At one level, it highlights the continuing ambiguity of race in the New Testament portion of the Bible. At another level, it confronts us today with a challenge to search for more adequate modes of hermeneutics by which the New Testament can be demonstrated as relevant to people of the Third World even as it stands locked into a socio-religious framework of the Graeco-Roman world. Of all of the mandates which confront the Church in the world today, the mandate of world community predicated on a renewed commitment to pluralism and the attendant acknowledgement of the integrity of all racial groups constitute an urgent agenda for Bible scholars and the laity alike. It is an agenda far too long nelected in the vast array of Euro-centric theological and ecclesial traditions which continue to marginalise people of colour throughout the world today.

Notes

1. Ronald E. Clements, s.v. 'gôy' *TDOT* II pp. 426-429.

2. S. D. Goitein *Jews and Arabs: Their Contacts Through the Ages* (New York 1964) pp. 19-21.

3. Αἰθίοψ (burnt-face): the most frequent translation of *CUSH* found in the LXX, designating usually Africans of dark pigmentation and Negroid features, used as early as Homer [*Odyssey* 19. 246ff.]. While Αἰθίοψ in ancient biblical and classical texts refers specifically to Ethiopians, the term also identifies Africans, regardless of race. Frank M. Snowden, Jr. *Blacks in Antiquity* (Cambridge, Mass. 1975) pp. 118-119.

4. G. E. Mendenhall employs the term secularisation in this sense. *Idem.* s.v. 'Election' *IDB* II p. 77.

5. Martin Noth *A History of Pentateuchal Traditions*, trans. Bernhard W. Anderson (Chico, California 1981) pp. 12-13, 28 and the translator's supplement pp. 262-263. Otto Eissfeldt *The Old Testament: An Introduction* (New York 1965) p. 184.

6. D. Harvey *IDB* IV p. 311.

7. The post-exilic priestly (P) redaction accounts for the order Shem, Ham, Japheth (omitting Canaan) in Gen. 10:1 as well as for the inversion of this order in the subsequent verses, e.g., Gen. 10:2 the sons of Japheth, Gen. 10:6 the sons of Ham, and Gen. 10:21 'To Shem also, the father of all the children of Eber (Hebrew)'.

8. Contra B. W. Anderson's note in *The New Oxford Annotated Bible* (RSV) p. 179: 'The term Cushite apparently (*sic*) includes Midianites and other Arabic peoples (Hab. 3:7).'

C

9. Ephraim Isaac 'Genesis, Judaism and the "Sons of Ham" ' *Slavery and Abolition:* A Journal of Comparative Studies 1, No. 1 (May 1980) 3-17.

10. Sergew Hable Sellassie *Ancient and Medieval Ethiopian History to 1270* (Addis Ababa 1972) p. 96; R. A. Morrisey *Colored People in Bible History* (Hammond, Ind. 1925); Edward Ullendorf *Ethiopia and the Bible* (London 1968) pp. 6-8.

11. F. M. Snowden pp. 115-117; Cheikh Anta Diop *The African Origin of Civilization:* Myth or Reality? trans. Mercer Cook (New York) pp. 220-221; Sir Alan Gardiner *Egypt of the Pharaohs* (New York 1974) [1961], p. 450.

12. Gerhard von Rad *Old Testament Theology* trans. D. M. G. Stalker (New York 1962) p. 7 and II p. 322.

13. *Ibid.* I pp. 118, 178; Horst Seebass, s.v. 'bachar' *TDOT* II 78; G. E. Mendenhall p. 76.

14. H. Seebass p. 82.

15. *Ibid.* p. 83.

16. So, G. E. Mendenhall p. 79; G. F. Moore *Judaism* II (Cambridge 1932) p. 95. But cf. Rashi's Commentary *Deuteronomy* trans. M. Rosenbaum et al. (New York) pp. 56, 195.

17. von Rad I pp. 178, 223.

18. H. Seebass p. 78.

19. G. F. Moore, as quoted in note 16.

20. Rudolf Bultmann *Theology of the New Testament* I (London 1965 [52]) p. 97.

21. (LXX) Isa. 43:20 τὸ γένος μού τὸ ἐκλεκτόν = M.T. *ammî běhîrî.*

22. W. Bauer *A Greek-English Lexicon of the New Testament* trans. and ed. W. E. Arndt and F. W. Gingrich (Chicago 1957) s.v. 'ἐκλεκτός' p. 242.

23. In I Clem. V. 7, 'the limits of the west' (ἐπὶ τὸ τέρμα τῆς δύσεως) designates Spain (or Rome): *Apostolic Fathers* trans. Kirsopp Lake I, Loeb Classical Library (Cambridge, Mass. 1975) p. 16. Cf. Rom. 15:28; Ernst Käsemann *Commentary on Romans* trans. and ed. Geoffrey W. Bromiley (Grand Rapids 1980) p. 402.

24. Luke's Acts of the Apostles outlines this schema quite decidedly: Jerusalem (Acts 2), Antioch (Acts 12), Athens (Acts 17) and Rome (Acts 28). See: Werner Georg Kümmel *Introduction to the New Testament* Rev. English Edition, trans. Howard C. Kee (Nashville 1975) pp. 164f.

25. Vincent Taylor *The Gospel According to St Mark* (New York 1966) p. 598; *The Passion in Mark* ed. Werner H. Kelber (Philadelphia 1976) pp. 120n, 155, 166.

26. The good reputations of the centurion in Luke 7:2ff and Cornelius the centurion in Acts 10:1, 22 are intentional designs by Luke: F. J. Foakes Jackson and Kirsopp Lake *The Acts of the Apostles* IV (Grand Rapids 1979) p. 112; Ernst Haenchen *The Acts of the Apostles* (Oxford 1971) pp. 346, 349.

27. E. Haenchen p. 309.

28. *Ibid.* p. 314.

29. *Ibid.* p. 315. Similarly: Martin Hengel *Acts and the History of Earliest Christianity* (Philadelphia 1980) p. 79.

30. Luke 1:3; Acts 1:1. See further: Hans Conzelmann *The Theology of St Luke* trans. Geoffrey Buswell (New York 1960) pp. 138-141 and Richard J. Cassidy *Jesus. Politics and Society* (Maryknoll, N.Y. 1978) pp. 128-130.

31. Notably the Pastorals and I Peter cf. Rom. 13:1-5.

Johannes Brosseder

The World Council of Churches' Programme to Combat Racism

RIGHT FROM the official beginnings of the ecumenical movement earlier this century there has been preoccupation with the problem of racism. In the brief surveys that have recently been published by John May[1] and Ans van der Bent[2] attention has rightly been drawn to this point. A prominent place is occupied especially by J. H. Oldham's book *Christianity and the Race Problem*, which appeared in 1926, as well as by the condemnations of Nazi racism and anti-Semitism[3] made within the ecumenical movement between 1933 and 1945. The first plenary assembly of the World Council of Churches held in Amsterdam in 1948 was aware that it was still concerned with this latter question, as is shown by the report of the committee dealing with the subject of the Christian approach to the Jews, even if the conference's conclusions were formulated in such a way as to remain open to a general perspective when the assembly came out against the flagrant violation of human rights through discrimination on grounds of race, colour, culture or political conviction.

1. DEVELOPMENT SINCE AMSTERDAM

A milestone in the development that was eventually to lead to the Programme to Combat Racism was the second plenary assembly of the World Council of Churches held at Evanston in 1954. The separation of people on grounds of race, colour or ethnic origin was solemnly condemned as contrary to the gospel and to the essential nature of the Christian Church. This condemnation explicitly included those churches in which such forms of separation existed: this was along the same lines as the public avowal already made by the churches of the ecumenical movement of not having done enough in the struggle against Nazi anti-Semitism. One of the chief problems of social justice with regard to racial or ethnic tensions was described as guaranteeing *everyone* the free exercise of civil rights and genuine participation in government at all levels. A special department of the World Council of Churches was called for to deal specifically with racial and ethnic conflicts and tensions. But some years were to pass before anything actually happened to put this into effect.

In 1960 a consultation took place at Cottesloe near Johannesburg between a racially mixed delegation from the World Council of Churches and South African member churches of the WCC. This concerned itself with the racial problems of southern Africa and drew up a declaration that was approved by 80 per cent of the South African participants. It recalled the rights of the Black population to land ownership as well as equal rights for Black people in the world of work, in education and in government. Among many other things it stressed that a ban on racially mixed marriages could not be justified on the basis of Scripture. While national values deserved understanding and respect as a means of self-realisation, the danger should not be overlooked of the nation replacing God as the absolute value. The Church's role could merely consist of helping directly national movements towards a just and suitable outcome.

After this Cottesloe declaration the three Dutch Reformed Churches in South Africa walked out of the World Council of Churches. This showed how difficult it was to try at the ecumenical level to help towards the solution of the race question. The third plenary assembly of the World Council of Churches, held at New Delhi in 1961, reaffirmed the 1954 Evanston declaration and, despite the difficulties that had become obvious, welcomed the establishment of a special secretariat within the WCC to concern itself with racial and ethnic problems. But once again a number of years had to pass before something could actually be done to put this into effect.

In 1963 the Central Committee of the WCC met at Rochester, N.Y. Here it was directly confronted with the march to Washington of Martin Luther King and his movement. Influenced by this non-violent march, the Central Committee of the WCC at its meeting in Rochester drew up a statement in which the churches in the United States and in South Africa were called on to intensify their efforts towards a peaceful solution of the race problem. In 1964 the US National Council of Churches of Christ asked the WCC for theological assistance for a project intended to serve reconciliation between the races in the Mississippi delta. In meeting this request the WCC pointed out that the race problem was world wide and that all Christians are bound to help solve it.

In the same year a consultation on Christians and race relations in southern Africa was held at Kitwe, Zambia, by the South African Institute of Race Relations and the Mindolo Ecumenical Foundation under the sponsorship of the Church and Society division of the WCC. This occupied itself with the following subjects: the churches' involvement in the race question, the growing trend away from non-violence towards the use of violence, and models of a solution in the economic structures of society. In 1966 the conference on Church and Society held in Geneva aroused a world-wide echo. At it ethnocentricity in the churches was rejected and Christians were urged to resist the myth of racial superiority and inferiority. Equal participation by all racial and ethnic groups in the life of the society they lived in was called for. The realisation that the white race dominated the world economically and politically and that therefore authentic human community was not really possible either within nations or between them led to the demand for this domination to be brought to an end. In this context reconciliation could not simply amount to a sentimental harmonisation of the parties to the conflict but demanded rather identification with the oppressed and active support for them in the struggle for dignity, freedom and justice for all. If Christians refused to take part in this struggle they would be disobeying God's summons in history.

This conference did not fail to have its effect on the fourth plenary assembly of the WCC held at Uppsala in 1968. This assembly too condemned racism as a flagrant violation of Christian faith. Racism denied the effectiveness of the reconciling work of Jesus Christ by whose love all human differences lost their divisive meaning; racism further denied the humanity shared by men and women generally as well as the belief that all men and women are made in the image of God; and finally racism falsely stated that we found our significance in our racial identity rather than in Jesus Christ. Uppsala went on to point to the entanglement of racism with economics and politics. From this it deduced the necessity of helping the victims of racism both economically and politically and above all with regard to a change in the existing economic and political structures in order to guarantee the equal participation of all in economic and political life. This also meant intensified involvement and commitment on the part of the mass media as well as guaranteeing the equality of everyone in the field of education and training.

The assembly stated that the development of an immediate programme was urgently demanded in order to provide guidance for the WCC and its member churches in the oppressive business of racism. The view of the assembly was that such a programme (a) should occupy itself with the development and present state of the problem of racism in the various parts of the world, including its manifestation in political and economic life, with studies of South Africa, the United States and Australia being especially desirable; (b) consultations on this subject should be held at regional and international level; (c) an advisory service should be set up to make available advice from experts in different Church and secular bodies; (d) the churches' judgment and experience should be communicated to various international bodies, particularly the United Nations; (e) investigations into potential areas of crisis should be prepared in order to make it possible for the churches and the secular authorities to try to prevent the growth of tensions with racial causes; (f) projects and schemes of joint action should be developed; (g) materials should be provided for educating the masses in questions of racism; and finally (h) within the general secretariat of the WCC a secretariat directed towards combating racism should be set up and an ecumenical commission should be appointed to watch over it.

This practical proposal by the Uppsala assembly led in 1969 to the well-known WCC consultation on racism that was held in Notting Hill, London, from 19 to 24 May that year. This consultation decided to recommend the following steps to the WCC: (1) the WCC and its member churches should impose economic sanctions on companies, organisations and institutions that go in for manifest racism; (2) a determined effort should be made to persuade governments for their part to impose such economic sanctions; (3) the churches should support the principle of 'repatriation' to exploited peoples and countries, which would involve the churches in having to share in such reparations on account of their having taken part in exploitation: both would be necessary to restore a just equilibrium of economic power in the world; (4) the WCC should set up an organisation with adequate resources to be able to accomplish the elimination of racism; (5) the UNESCO report on racism should be distributed among member churches to enable Christians to understand the struggle against racism that is required; (6) the WCC should act as a co-ordinating centre for the variety of strategies undertaken by the churches in the struggle against racism in South Africa; and finally (7) if everything else is of no avail the Church and the churches should support resistance movements, including revolutions, that receive aid towards overcoming the political and economic tyranny that is made possible by racism.

2. PROGRAMME TO COMBAT RACISM

These recommendations led to actual plans to set up the Programme to Combat Racism, which was approved by the Central Committee of the WCC at its meeting at Canterbury in August 1969. The Central Committee ratified the recommendations of the Notting Hill consultation and decided on a five-year mandate for an ecumenical Programme to Combat Racism. At Arnoldshain in 1970 the executive committee of the WCC approved the criteria to be followed in disbursing funds worked out by the International Advisory Committee for the Programme to Combat Racism. The criteria to be followed were: preference should be given to supporting organisations that fought against racism rather than welfare organisations that ameliorated the effects of racism and received aid from other divisions of the WCC; the focus of aid should be to raise the level of awareness of those suffering from racial oppression and to strengthen their opportunities for organisation; the necessity was further underlined of supporting liberation movements in those places where the struggle was at its most intense and where the means used could have the greatest effect; and, while the funds should not be used to purchase weapons, any check or supervision on this point was explicitly foregone. The first grants were made to movements and institutions in Australia, Great Britain, the Netherlands, Japan, Colombia, Zambia, Mozambique, Angola, Guinea-Bissau, South Africa, Namibia and Rhodesia (now Zimbabwe).

Since then the PCR has been marked by an increasingly practical emphasis. The inspiration may come from theological questions, but the chief attention is directed rather to economic, military, political, industrial and financial problems, above all in southern Africa. Mention should be made here of the meetings of the Central Committee of the WCC in Addis Ababa in 1971, in Utrecht in 1972, in West Berlin in 1974, in Geneva in 1976 and 1977, in Kingston, Jamaica, in 1979, and in Geneva in 1980. Mention should also be made of the Faith and Order consultation on 'Racism in theology and theology against racism' held at Geneva in 1975 as well as of the fifth plenary assembly of the World Council of Churches held at Nairobi in 1975. The question of the PCR's basic financial capital was discussed and it was originally decided it should be $500,000, later raised to $1,000,000; it was further decided in 1974 to disburse $300,000 annually from the fund towards the objects of the PCR. The subject of violence and non-violence was raised without it being possible to speak of a consensus on this within the World Council and its member churches.

An important role was played by the question of investment in southern Africa. At Utrecht in 1972 the Central Committee directed the WCC's finance committee and its director of finances to sell all existing shares immediately and not to make any future investment in undertakings that were directly concerned in investment or trade with one of the following countries: South Africa, Namibia, Rhodesia (as Zimbabwe then still was), Angola, Mozambique and Guinea-Bissau. Nor should any WCC funds be deposited in banks that maintained direct commercial links with these countries. At the same time all member churches, Christian organisations and individual Christians outside southern Africa were asked to do everything in their power, including exerting influence as shareholders and disposing of shareholdings, to force undertakings to withdraw their investments in these countries and to cease trading with them. There may have been an explicit welcome for proposals from the Evangelical church in Germany, for example, to bring about racial justice in southern Africa by means of reforms in the context of a variety of approaches, but the withdrawal of investments should nevertheless now take place. In this context mention must also be made of the WCC's efforts to persuade large national and international banks to cease making loans to South Africa. The lengthy correspondence with the banks did not lead to any agreement on the questions raised. The fifth plenary assembly of the World Council of Churches in Nairobi went into the problem of racism in considerable detail and presented a very impressive synthesis of the complexity of this problem (section V: structures of injustice and struggles for liberation) without, however, being able to say anything really fundamentally new. What, however, is worth noting is the attempt to be as down to earth as possible.

If so far southern Africa has been in the foreground of interest, in the 1980s attention should be directed more intensely to other countries as well, especially in Asia, as was demanded by the Central Committee at its meeting in Kingston, Jamaica, in 1979.

The Programme to Combat Racism has provoked some very fierce argument in many of the World Council's member churches. The subject of the use of violence and the procedure followed in disbursing funds have been and are particularly controversial.

What is not a matter of controversy in the churches is that no form of racism can be reconciled with the fundamentals of Christian faith. But when it comes to how racism may best be opposed opinions diverge very widely. This is shown among other things by a carefully worded memorandum issued by the Evangelical church in Germany on 6 November 1978 as well as by this church's considered proposals for the process of consultation about the church's participation in the fight against racism in the 1980s. The anxieties felt in this church are understandable against the background of recent German history, inasmuch as the Programme to Combat Racism involves fundamental questions of the Church's political mandate and political ethics that have been discussed in Germany with particular awareness in view of the Church's failure to make an adequate stand in the Nazi period.

For the rest these subjects are controversial when they are discussed elsewhere throughout the world. If one reads the statements of the Programme to Combat Racism and concentrates merely on the practical sections, leaving aside the theological considerations, one cannot always resist the impression that here one merely finds repeated what has long since been said elsewhere, for example in the United Nations, leaving undecided for the moment the question whether it has always been said rightly. In view of the practical realities of oppression and exploitation one hardly dares write such statements any longer. But they have to be written because concern for the gospel and concern for people's prosperity and well-being belong together. However, practical steps in the struggle against structural racism cannot yet enjoy that unambiguity that Christians expect to find in the eschaton towards which they are on their way.

As long as we are on our way, the various individual paths adopted remain a matter of controversy. That applies to every human action. But what ought not to be a matter of controversy is the universal relatedness to each other of Christians in the various different countries. They must not fail to account to each other for the particular path they happen to have taken. Whether among the churches enough attention is really paid to what the other person is doing and why cannot be decided here. But in any case it is thanks to the WCC that it has not let this subject, which has to be considered in the light of the gospel, be dropped and that it has brought up into the public consciousness of Christendom how on this question we live out our faith—along with all the controversy that attaches to actual particular decisions in the economic and political sphere.

Translated by Robert Nowell

Notes

1. John May 'Sprache der Einheit—Sprach der Zwietracht. Der Rassismus als Testfall ökumenischer Kommunikation' in Peter Lengsfeld *Ökumenische Theologie. Ein Arbeitsbuch* (Stuttgart 1980) pp. 251-284 (on Oldham's book p. 271).

2. *World Council of Churches' Statement and Actions on Racism 1948-1979* ed. Ans van der Bent (Geneva 1980).

3. I have basically relied on the following sources and writings: *World Council of Churches' Statements and Actions on Racism 1948-1979* ed. Ans van der Bent (Geneva 1980); 'Ökumenischer Rat der Kirchen (Programm Zur Bekämpfung des Rassismus *Zur Frage der Investitionen im südlichen Afrika* (Geneva 1973); *Bankkredite für die Apartheid und der Ökumenische Rat der Kirchen*, translated by Otmar Schulz (Frankfurt-am-Main 1978) (English original Geneva 1977); John Downing *Now You Do Know: an independent report on racial oppression in Britain for submission to a World Council of Churches' consultation* (no date or place of publication 1980); World Council of Churches' Programme to Combat Racism *PCR-Information: Reports and*

Background Papers No. 1 (Geneva 1979); Ökumenischer Rat der Kirchen (Zentralausschuss) *Kirchliche Antirassismusarbeit in den 80er Jahren*, document No. 17, No. 33 (Geneva 1980); Barbara Rogers 'Race: No Peace without Justice' in *Churches Confront the Mounting Racism of the 1980s* (published by the World Council of Churches, Geneva 1980); *Racism in Children's and School Textbooks* (Geneva 1980); Erika Fuchs *Ökumenischer Rat der Kirchen. Antirassismus-Programm 1969-1979* ed. Peter Karner (aktuelle Reihe No. 16) (Vienna no date (1979?)); Hanfried Krüger *Ökumenische Bewegung*, supplementary numbers of the *Ökumenische Rundschau* Nos. 3/4, 12/13, 28, 29 (Stuttgart 1966 onwards); C. Meyers-Herwartz *Die Rezeption des Antirassismusprogramms in der EKD* (Stuttgart 1979); 'Memorandum on the relationship of the Evangelical Church in Germany to the World Council of Churches, with special reference to the Programme to Combat Racism and its special fund (approved by the Council of the EKD on 6 November 1978) in *Ökumenische Rundschau* 28 (1979) pp. 43-51; *Erfahrungen, Einsichten, Vorschläge. Überlungen aus der EKD für den Beratungsprozess über die Beteiligung der Kirchen an der Bekämpfung des Rassismus in den 80er Jahren. Antwort auf die Fragen des ÖRK von 19.11.1979* (Typescript, Evangelical Church in Germany 1980). Indications of further literature can be found in *Internationale Ökumenische Bibliographie*, ed. Johannes Brosseder, vol. 10/11, (Munich/Mainz 1977), and vol. 12/13/14 (Munich/Mainz 1980) under the relevant headings.

Roger-Henri Guerrand

The Catholic Church's Struggle Against Racialism

EVERY FORM of racialism, even the most limited, eats away at the heart of Christianity and erodes charity, because its implied contempt and mistrust of one's neighbour is in effect an attack against that person. During the middle ages, Christians often persecuted the Jews and the Moors, but this violence was directed not against their race, but against their 'infidelity'. At that time, no national restrictions were imposed on the movements of peoples and on appointment to high positions in the Church.

The time of racial contempt really began in the sixteenth century with the Spanish conquest of America. Pope Paul III was made aware of what was happening there by the Dominicans and especially by the missionary priest Bartolomé de las Casas, who devoted his life to the defence of the Indians, and published, in May and June 1537, a series of bulls reflecting for the first time the attitude of the sovereign pontiffs towards racial questions. A typical statement is: 'The enemy of the human race has suggested to some of his satellites that the idea should be disseminated in the world that the inhabitants of the West Indies and the southern continents . . . should be treated like animals devoid of reason and used exclusively for our profit and service, on the pretext that they do not share the Catholic faith and are not capable of adopting it. As the unworthy vicar of Jesus Christ, we regard the Indians as true men who are not only capable of adopting the Christian faith, but who also aspire to it.' Because racialism has its origin in the demon, as Paul III openly declared in this statement, it can only be an occasion of mortal sin.

This important text was completed in the following century by Pope Alexander VII's instruction to the vicars apostolic who were about to set off for the Chinese kingdoms of Tonkin and Cochin-China. This document contains a magnificent proclamation of Christian respect for other cultures: 'Do not try in any way, even in the form of advice, to make the people whom you have evangelised change their rites, customs or way of life, except in those cases in which those factors are absolutely incompatible with the Christian religion and good principles. Would there in fact be anything more absurd than the introduction of characteristics peculiar to France, Spain or Italy into China? That is not what you have to preach! You have to preach faith—that faith which is not only willing to accept every rite and custom that does not contradict it, but also goes so far as to protect them. Do not try, then, to replace the practices of those peoples with European customs and take the greatest possible care to adapt yourseves to them.'

31

In the countries themselves, however, two missionary tactics had already been applied and were to be used concurrently until at least the middle of the twentieth century. The first meant that conversion became a total renewal involving a complete break with the original religious, social and political institutions. This system was effectively adopted by the Spanish religious working in South America.

The process of evangelisation consisted first of all in gathering the Indians in villages—a practice which was in itself in formal opposition to their traditional way of life. It is true that no attempt was made by the missionaries, who expressed themselves only in the language of their believers, to make the people 'Spanish', but these 'reductions' were doomed to fail because of the minority claim that they implied. This claim, after all, meant that the foreign religious would remain indefinitely—since they refused to train a native clergy—and that the native Christian converts had to break both with the rest of their own people and with the Europeans, who believed that they were forbidden to live in the missionary villages, which extended as far as California.

It is not at all easy to measure the dose of racialism contained in this form of paternalism, but it was in any case revealed when the Jesuits themselves admitted in South America—at least in practice—that slavery was legitimate. Their colleges and universities certainly resorted to it.

Victor-Daniel Bonilla has shown how harmful this system of reductions has been in his discussion of a modern example. In seventy years, from 1906 onwards, the Spanish Capuchins succeeded in destroying an Indian culture which had hitherto resisted white colonisation for four centuries.[1]

This desire to keep the coloured people in a state of dependence was also revealed in 1870 at the First Vatican Council, where, for the first time, fifteen of the twenty-two missionary bishops in the royalty of China were present, all European. They held special meetings to discuss their problems and agreed to declare that the Chinese priests—at that time two hundred in number to two hundred white missionaries—ought to be treated as 'pupils and sons and not as equals and brothers'. It was in this way that the affairs of the Church in China were regulated without any of its Chinese members being present. It was necessary to wait for Pius XII before a Chinese bishop could become a member of the Sacred College.

The second missionary tactic—and the only one that really conformed to the Roman instructions—was based on the idea that the new convert had no need to break with his previous way of life because no race or people was in fact totally wrong or sinful. The Recollects, Jesuits and Sulpicians in Canada therefore proclaimed that the Indians were true sons of Jesus Christ and that their way of life was superior to that of western Christians, which was exactly what Bartolomé de las Casas had been saying. To find the disinterested charity which had filled the early Christians, one had to go to the Indians.

At the juridical level, Cardinal Richelieu, the founder of the 'Company of the Hundred Associates', the group which had the task of building up the New France, regarded every convert Indian as entirely French. He declared that 'Christian savages can come to France when they think fit and acquire, bequeath, inherit and receive legacies and gifts as much as native Frenchmen without having been granted naturalisation.'

At the beginning of the reign of Louis XIV in 1664, the 'Society of Foreign Missions', the declared aim of which was to promote the training of native clergy, was established in Paris. In this context, it is also worth recalling the 'respectful' way in which the Jesuits hoped to succeed in evangelising China. They became excellent linguists, even more skilled than the mandarins themselves, and in this way gained the trust of the emperors, who seriously entertained the idea of the mass conversion of their subjects to Catholicism. This decision was blocked by the reluctance of the Chinese to abandon the worship of their ancestors. This was used as a pretext for the Jesuits' enemies to sabotage their campaign by enlisting the sympathy of the popes, who were unable to grasp the great importance of what was involved.

There can be no doubt that many nineteenth-century missionaries were so influenced by the imperialistic ideas of their environment in Europe that they behaved more as representatives of their own original countries than as representatives of Christ. At the same time, however, there were others who acted quite differently. Cardinal Lavigerie's White Fathers, for example, adapted themselves so closely to the people of North Africa and their way of life that they even combated slavery.

From 1920 onwards, Benedict XV began to combat, as his predecessors had done, nationalistic tendencies in missionary work and the racialism that follows nationalism like a shadow. In his encyclical, *Maximum illud*, and his instruction, *Quo efficacius*, he reasserted the need for missionaries to be careful not to spread the use of their own language among the natives, to avoid all attempts to introduce laws and practices that were particular to their own country and to refrain from promoting trade with their own nation.

In his first encyclical, *Summi Pontificatus*, of 1939, Pius XII returned to the theme of fundamental respect for all cultures. In it, he said, for example: 'The Church of Christ cannot and does not think of attacking or underestimating the special characteristics that every people preserves with jealous piety and understandable pride and regards as a precious inheritance. Its aim is supernatural unity in a universal love that is both felt and practised and not an exclusively external, superficial and therefore weakening uniformity.'

At that time, there was a strong revival of racialism and anti-Semitism in Europe. Hitler's ideas, as worked out in *Mein Kampf*, aroused echoes even in France. During the Abyssinian War of 1935, when the League of Nations condemned Italy, a manifesto on 'The Defence of the West and Peace in Europe' went the rounds among French intellectuals. Eight hundred and fifty signatures were collected, including those of sixteen members of the Académie Française and twelve other members of various branches of the Institute. These men in high office did not hesitate to utter the following words of caution: 'Geneva is placing what is superior and what is inferior, what is civilised and what is barbarous on the same footing of equality. We now have clearly before us the results of this frenzy to make everything equal and to confuse everything with everything else. It is in the name of equality that those sanctions were formulated which, in an attempt to check the conquest of one of the most backward countries in the world in order to civilise it, would not hesitate to unleash a universal war and unite all anarchy and all disorder against a nation in which some of the great virtues of mankind have, in the past fifteen years, been affirmed, increased, organised and strengthened.'

This text, which would be well worth analysing in detail, bears clear witness to a deep spiritual disturbance even among such intellectuals and 'humanists' as the subtle and refined Jean Giraudoux. There was in fact at that time a widespread climate of general resignation in the face of the seduction exercised by fascism—as represented in France, for example, by the team that produced the publication *Je suis partout*—and an attitude which made racialism and anti-Semitism the basis of a new view of the world.

It was in this climate that Pius XI published, on 14 March 1937, an encyclical on the situation of the Catholic Church in Germany. The pope recalled with great force in this document that 'the entire human race is one great universal race'. A year later, all the rectors of Catholic seminaries and universities received precise instructions concerning the need to combat a number of carefully listed and described racialist propositions. The cardinal archbishops of Malines, Paris and Milan and the patriarch of Lisbon published a declaration in the same vein and the vice-principal of the Institut Catholique of Paris, Mgr Bressolles, Fr de la Brière, Robert d'Harcourt and Albert de Lapparent also vigorously attacked the fascist ideology in a series of lectures on 'Racialism and Christianity'.

The German Church, however, was infected by the racialist and anti-Semitic virus even before Hitler came to power. Cardinal Faulhaber, who was later to become Archbishop of Munich declared, for example, at a great meeting of German Catholics in 1922: 'We must speak quite openly: it does not matter whether one is the eldest or the youngest daughter of the Church, no one has the right to send pagans and Muslims to protect the civilisation of Catholic states.' This statement contained a clear reference to the colonial troops of the French army of the Rhine. Another example of the same kind of thinking can also unfortunately be attributed to Cardinal Faulhaber, who took it on himself to deny—from the pulpit—the rumour that was spreading at the time in Germany that Pius XI may have had a Jewish origin.

During the occupation, in France, Holland and Belgium, the Catholic hierarchy remained faithful to the teachings of Pius XI. The fact is that his successor did not speak as plainly as he had. Various attempts have been made, often by means of detailed analysis, to interpret the enigmatic attitude of Pius XII, but no one has so far succeeded in reaching an understanding.

Be that as it may, the popes who have followed Pius XII have always been anxious to distinguish between the Church's message and that of the West and to affirm the dignity and equality of all men. In recent years, there have been many references in papal documents to these problems. In the same way, although they have taken a long time to grasp the nettle, the bishops in the southern states of America have at last begun to speak out against those of their flock who favour segregation. Other similar cases are the declarations of Mgr Duval in his defence of the Muslims during the Algerian war and the statements condemning apartheid made by Church leaders in South Africa.

According to the centuries-old tradition of the Roman Church, the missionary task of spreading the Christian faith has always been regarded as supra-national, just as faith itself also transcends national boundaries. There is nowadays increasing respect for this principle in the Church, just as there is for the differences between peoples and nations. This principle has, in fact, become almost a dogma and the desire to transcend these differences in the unity of the mystical Body of Christ is affirmed as an ideal that can make an important contribution to peace in the world.

Translated by David Smith

Note

1. *Serfs de Dieu et maitres d'Indiens* (Paris 1972).

Deotis Roberts

A Creative Response to Racism: Black Theology

THE PURPOSE of this essay is to explore the historic roots of Black Theology. This is no mean assignment—it is an awesome task. It is clear that what we will be able to do within the limitations of space and time given to this task can be only exploratory and provisional. But it is a work that must be done and it is a privilege to begin so noble an endeavour.

Having said these things, we shall now indicate how we expect to approach our subject. First, we will suggest that the origins of Black Theology are hidden in the oral tradition of Black religious experience. Second, we shall illustrate this assumption by folkloric references in sermons and other folk expressions. Third, we will trace the ideological basis for Black Theology. Fourth, we will look at Black Theology itself as a formal programme with special reference to its Method and Content. We will conclude with a critical assessment of the past and present status of the movement. Having charted out an ambitious course, the task now begins.

1. ORIGINS OF BLACK THEOLOGY IN THE ORAL TRADITION

What we now call Black Theology is about a decade old. When we make this assertion, it is necessary to indicate what we mean by Black Theology. What we do not mean should be first; for this will set our definition in its proper context. We do not have in mind basic religious beliefs which are abundant in the oral or written traditions of Blacks, though elements of Black Theology are found there. Neither do we have in mind a popular or journalistic notion of 'Black Theology' which turns out to be an expression of Black folk religious beliefs. What we do have in mind is a formal and systematic interpretation of a creed of doctrine worked out by persons who are practising theologians with the knowledge and skills of this discipline. Furthermore, Black Theology is thus a term for the expression of a faith for Black Christians who belong to congregations of Christians. It is an expression of the Christian Faith in the Black experience for all Black Christians—including those in white denominations. But it is a theology which has special reference to those Blacks who are deeply embedded in the Black congregations in Black communities. Black Theology is essentially Black Church Theology. Here we speak of the centre and context of Black Theology. It is, however, compelled to enter into conversation or dialogue beyond this foundational setting.

With this preliminary look at our subject, we may now explore somewhat the origins of Black Theology in the oral tradition. This tradition goes back to Africa as W. E. B. DuBois reminds us in his classic discourse on 'Black spirituality'.[1] Africa, as we know, has much of its cultural history encouched in an oral tradition. African religions are not religions of the Book as are Semitic religions and many Middle Eastern and Asian religions. African religious beliefs are not easily understood by means of western logic and metaphysics. Scholars, Black and White, whose sole intellectual equipment consists of the historical-critical method of biblical exegesis or whose thought-structures are shaped by Aristotelian logic or Platonic metaphysics are ill-equipped to unlock the message of the African background to Afro-American thought and belief.[2]

It is obvious that since we have such tribal diversity among Africans and their religious systems, phenomenology of religion, social psychology and anthropology as well as ethno-history are indispensable tools of investigation. C. H. Long, as a Black historian of religion,[3] and Joseph R. Washington,[4] as a sociologist of religion, have done some creative excavations in these areas.

2. THE ROOTS OF BLACK THEOLOGY

The indigenous base for Black Theology is found in our oral ethno-history. It is found in the exhortation of Black preachers and the simple folktales of unschooled Black People. It is found in popular literature and in classic prose, poetry and drama. In a word, the roots of Black Theology are deeply embedded in the soil of Black culture.

Dr Martin L. King, Jr., recalled that he walked beside an elderly woman in the Selma March. He inquired of her if she was tired of walking. Her reply was: 'My feets am tired, but my soul am rested.' In the midst of great suffering we have been blessed with a sense of humour, 'the gift of laughter'. We have been able to rejoice in the midst of tears.

John J. Jasper (1812-93) was a slave during his youth. A fellow slave taught him to read. He started reading out of the *New York Spelling Book* until he was able to read the Bible. Within months he was converted and soon after that he was called to preach. He was no doubt a biblical fundamentalist innocent of any natural scientific knowledge. But his sermon 'De Sun Do Move' is a theological credo in itself. He makes no reservation in affirming the creative and redemptive purposes of God. God is Creator, Redeemer and Judge.

'My Lord is great! He rules in de heavens, in de earth and down under de ground. . . .'[5]

The explorations of the Black Theologian into folk materials is rewarding. But it must be done in such manner that the theologian may get in touch with the people who are in touch with God. The most valiant attempt to get at this folk base for 'Black Beliefs' has radiated through the works of Henry Mitchell.

My work in this area has been mainly encouched in my study of folklore.[6]

This study is not so much theology but literary criticism and phenomenology of religion. The theologian must consciously lean away from this material with his convictions until the sources speak to him. Once the theologian is able to describe what he has discovered in the phenomenon of the mass Black religious experience he can properly begin the hermeneutical task of interpreting and communicating what he has found.

3. THE IDEOLOGICAL BASIS FOR BLACK THEOLOGY

Black Theology is often rejected both for being uprooted from Black folk religious experience, and its claim to be a programme of formal systematic theology. Ideas have consequences. Thought is the basis of action no less than it is for reflection. Anyone studying the social upheavals in the Third World during the post-colonial period may make this assertion on hard evidence. We make a serious mistake when we posit Black religious experience in the affections alone.

A holistic approach to the existing individual requires that the head, heart and will be moved by a source of belief. Here we do not argue for the emotional quality of soul. Here we are concerned more about the cognitive as well as the volitional content of the soul quality of Black experience. Knowledge can be intuitive as well as rational. The existentialists insist that 'truth is subjectivity'—it is participation of the knower in what is known. Most African/Black thinkers appear to assume an existentialist posture. Howard Thurman, the Black mystic-poet-religious philosopher *par excellence*, is a sterling example.

But an equally important characteristic of Black thought is its sensitivity to community. *Ujamma*, 'familyhood' or a network of kinship ties informs the best in African/Afro-American thought and practice. We have only begun to unpack the significance of the image of the Black extended family for a doctrine of the Church in Black Theology. This is crucial not merely for the depth and intimacy of fellowship, but for the political and social mission of a fellowship made up of an oppressed people seeking liberation here and now. This is a way of suggesting that spirituality, fellowship, ethics and social action are all bound up with a theological exploration of communalism in the African connection of Black churches.

Thus far it is the prophetic vision that has been more clearly lifted up in Black Theology. Thus it builds more securely upon the radicalism in Black religious history. There is a spiritual component in Black religious experience which has been virtually neglected in the quest for a more 'political' message.

Here we will be brief in presenting some evidence for the assertion of 'radicalism' in Black religious history. This is not to ignore the 'compensatory' or reactionary characteristics of our history. The works by S. Stuckey[7] and R. F. Betts[8] trace by means of documents and interpretation 'the ideology of blackness'. Stuckey has presented and interpreted such seminal documents as 'The Ethiopian Manifesto' by Robert Alexander Young; 'The Appeal' by David Walker; 'Address to the Slaves' by Henry Highland Garnet and 'The Political Destiny of the Colored Race' by Martin R. Delany. Betts has brought to this discussion materials from Edward W. Blyden, Marcus Garvey and Malcolm X, to mention only a few. What we meet here and elsewhere is a series of instalments upon a whole tradition of Black radicalism in nationalistic 'manifestos' providing a pattern of reflection upon ideologies of Black liberation. What is remarkable is the manner in which religious convictions inform this entire tradition. Religion behind this tradition is derived from Christian and non-Christian sources. Black ecumenism growing out of the thirst for freedom has never been provincial. It transcends sectarianism as it focuses upon liberation. It provides a basis for an 'operational unity' against a common foe—racism—and for a unified goal—liberation.

Black religionists, especially ministers, were deeply supportive of abolitionism, the convention movement and economic development and moral uplift in the nineteenth century. Religion has been a factor in the history of the NAACP as well as the Harlem Literary Renaissance. 'Black power' was manifest in the labour involvement of A. Philip Randolph and the ministry of Adam Clayton Powell, Jr. All of these currents of thought and activism filtered into the Civil Rights/Integration period which reached its nadir in the decade from 1954-65. The history of the Black power/conscious movement built on these ideological and activistic foundations. The current approach to Black liberation may be reformist and not revolutionary, but it plugs into this same history of thought and faith among Blacks. The Black Theologian, as interpreter, must bring the deeper understanding of the gospel to this sustained push for freedom incorporated in our history. We affirm that faith in God has brought us 'thus far on the way' and this faith will lead us on.

Before moving rapidly into the evaluation of existing programmes of Black Theology, we need to look at the recent historical antecedents which gave rise to this programme. We see three distinct and yet continuous ideological stages, reaching from 1954 to the present. First from 1954-65, we meet the Civil Rights/Integration stage. Second, from 1966-72, we encounter the Black consciousness/Black power phase. And, finally, from 1973 to the present we entered the 'political' involvement period. The dates are rudely conceived by a non-historian. They are approximate and are derived from an experience of the flow of a historical span in which I have been personally involved. You may question the dates, but will need to reckon with what happened and its meaning for Black people. My chronology may be questioned, but my preoccupation is with the 'kairotic' content of this history.

Black religion and Black Theology saw Black consciousness/power in a special way. We saw the affirmation of blackness as leading to a re-definition of our own being as persons and as a people. Through this re-definition of our existence we found a way to self-respect and self-determination. We no longer accepted the image of ourselves in the White mind. Theologians and churchmen among us saw this Black consciousness/power movement in its cultural/historical context as a part of the entire religious heritage of Blacks. Furthermore, as we re-read the Bible and re-conceived the Faith we were able to see more clearly what God through Christ is doing in the world to make life more human.

Finally, the last and the continuing stage of the Black movement which theologians of the Black experience need to consider is what Preston Williams correctly refers to as 'reformist' rather than 'revolutionary'. This came to me in a conversation, though it reflects the spirit of much of his writing as well. More and more leadership among Blacks coming out of the civil rights period as well as the Black power stage seems to be reformist. There is a turn towards 'political' involvement. We are not seeking integration or separation. We are affirming our ethnicity within a pluralistic culture. We are embracing the best from civil rights and Black power but using more and more the power acquired within the 'system' to make it more humane. Those who are privileged to acquire status and influence may no longer be acclaimed by the Black masses for their ascendency. They are now being held accountable to use their position of power and privilege to set their brothers and sisters free.

In the document *Gaudium et Spes* (the Church and the Modern World), Vatican II called the theologians of the Catholic Church to the task of reading the 'signs of the times'. Black Theologians will be irresponsible and unworthy if they do not see this as central to their task and programme.

4. BLACK THEOLOGY

There are two things to be discussed at this point, blackness and theology. 'Blackness' has to do with an awareness of belonging to the Afro-American heritage. It is far more than consciousness of a colour of skin. It has to do with a new self-definition, a different self-understanding and a sense of worth. It symbolises that our dignity as human beings is no longer at the mercy of the image of Blacks in the White mind.

'Black' is a 'dirty' word in our culture. It is defined by Webster as ugly, evil, fiendish and everything undesirable. We have re-defined this term and 'transvaluated' it. We have taken a word which is shameful, a badge of inferiority, of ostracism and shrouded it in a halo of glory. This is not unlike the arch symbol of our faith—the Cross. The 'curse' of the Cross has been translated by Christians into the ultimate salvific symbol of our Faith. Foolishness has been transformed into the very power and wisdom of God. Blackness has been re-defined in like manner into a meaningful symbol of Black Theologians. But Blackness associated with oppression is negative. It is that form which we desire to be delivered. Blackness is a whole set of experiences of Afro-Americans deeply embedded in their history and culture.

We are able now to accept our humanity as it is in God's creative and redemptive purposes. We are Sons of God. We are children of God. This is God's good pleasure. The way we understand our personhood and our peoplehood sets us upon a quest for a beloved community. We can now put in theological perspective our liberating quest.

Black Theology addresses itself to a liberating understanding of reconciliation. We understand the pain and wrath of God as well as His love and mercy. We see the revelation of the character of God as justice and power as well as love. God's providence is understood in relation to the crimes of history as well as in reference to personal transgressions. Jesus becomes a radical and He is understood as the Oppressed One or as a Suffering Slave because of his involvement in the liberation of the Oppressed. Reconciliation is not merely vertical, it is horizontal as well. It involves understanding what God is doing in the world to set men free and joining him in the liberation push. It means opposing power structures that dehumanise life. It involves a political, social justice understanding of the faith that resists the institutional and cultural manifestations of oppression based on race. Reconciliation does not exist apart from sharing power. It requires a new White consciousness that includes Cross-bearing, the willingness to accept all men as equals in a new relationship in which one gives up self-glory, the worship of white skin, and participation in the new humanity in which there are no slaves or masters but humans.

Black Theology is theological ethics. It has as its mission the humanising of life as well as the liberation of the oppressed. It must maintain a balance between liberation and reconciliation. In fact they exist together. The outlook of Black Theology is expressed in terms of hope. We are a people who have not only survived but have woven a living hope out of the crucible of suffering. While others are giving up because of corruption in places, we have moved beyond despair. We are seeking and acquiring political, economic and social power. While some theologians are still implying that we are not interested in 'winning', Black leaders and those who elect them are. We must not get out of touch with the people and especially when they may understand the faith better than we do. Almost to a man the Black elected officials are advocating the humanising of life for everyone. Most of them are conscious of being Black and are taking a strong stand for the liberation of Blacks but they are not seeking revenge on others. They are seeking a levelling of society, a sharing of power, goods and services, but liberation is in the context of togetherness on a higher level between equals. Theologians to these Black politicians who are delivering concrete benefits to Black people must address themselves to the direction of Black power and the humanising of White power, to the ends that are mutually beneficial to all people. Could it be that the legacy of Dr King or even that of Jesus is more present in the secular order than among the anointed? If Black Theology is to be more than an abstract enterprise for the edification of Black Theologians themselves it must begin to read the signs of the times to see what God's doing in the liberation struggle. These Black secular leaders appear to be strange prophets who are 'doers of the word and not hearers only'. They are acting as if they understand how love, justice and power mingle in the nature of God and in the Christian ethic; for they are working out a liberating approach to reconciliation in the social order. While some Black Theologians are talking about dying for freedom, these men are delivering bread and butter and providing employment and welfare checks in the language that the Black-poor trust and obey.

D

5. METHOD AND CONTENT OF BLACK THEOLOGY

The Black Theologian will find a method of discourse as his programme develops. At the outset he will be forced to develop his writing from a provisional method. Theology is based upon the certitude that emerges from careful reflection upon the revelation of God in human experience. Theology, on the other hand, is not founded upon a religion of reason. Faith has the priority. But faith is always seeking understanding. Black Theology, therefore, has to deal with the question of knowledge. The formula of a faith seeking understanding is the most satisfying position for the present writer.

After a provisional answer to the question of knowledge, one encounters the meaning of revelation. One can adopt a very limited view of the revelation of God to faith. If the revelation of God is limited to a Christo-centric view, then only those who 'know Christ' have a key to the revelation of God to faith. If, on the other hand, one allows a broader view of revelation which embraces God's unfolding of his mind and will in nature and history, then real encounter can take place with non-Christians at home and abroad. God's revelation is seen as manifest in the rising of the sun in the history of peoples, in the Bible as well as in the word made flesh. Christ can still be viewed as the 'Centre' or the 'Norm' of all revelation. We must, if we are truly committed to Christianity, assert that God has made himself known more completely in Jesus Christ than anywhere else. Black Theology has a special need for this kind of openness if it is to make significant contact with a broad-based Black religious nationalism on the homefront as well as traditional African religions abroad. This understanding of revelation opens up to secular forms of humanism which are involved in the Black liberation thrust.

God's revelation is towards the liberation of humans from all forms of injustice at the hands of fellow men. The revelation of God is met by the response of faith in the Christian. Liberation and reconciliation involve human and divine co-operation. We are labourers together with God towards a more humane order.

In this brief statement the writer has capsuled the working outline for a Black Theology of liberation and reconciliation. It is presented as a theology which is conscious of Blackness and yet open to all persons of good-will. It speaks to the matters of personal health and wholeness, but it is designed to uproot social evils and move the churches into the struggle for liberation and reconciliation.

6. CRITIQUE

Black Theology is a recent development as a formal programme of theology. It has yet to emerge as a seasoned project. The potential for a breakthrough in Black Theology is almost limitless if one reaches back into the riches of the Black religious heritage and forward into the challenges of an uncharted future while serving the present age.

Black Theology is a protest theology. It is a strong contemporary manifestation of the voice of the Old Testament prophets as well as the mission and message of Jesus against injustice and inhumanity. It is also a theology of culture drawing upon the rich heritage of peoples of African descent in the First and Third Worlds. There is deep spirituality in this tradition bound up with our ethnic existence and destiny. We must cultivate our communal or kinship ties in the way we do theology. Studies like Haley's *Roots* and Gutman's *Black Family* must be examined carefully and critically for they provide prospectives on our common heritage we will find useful in interpreting the faith to the Black churches and communities.

While keeping close to Christ as Centre, we must open up to the circumference of Pan-African spirituality. Indeed, our message of liberation must be peculiar to our

North American reality, but it must also reach into the situation of our kin in southern Africa. God reveals Himself in creation and providence on a cosmic scale at the same time that he makes Himself known uniquely and supremely in Jesus Christ. As Archbishop Temple puts it, 'God is revealed in the rising of the sun in the sky as He is in the raising of the Son from the dead'. Black Theology must partake of an ecumenical spirit in reference to non-Church sects and cults as well as non-Christian religious beliefs of brothers and sisters in a common struggle. While holding firmly to the faith of Christians, we must celebrate our common spirituality and develop an operational unity for Black liberation for all.

Perhaps our most important question quests in light of our religious and cultural heritage is to find thought-structures and the proper hermeneutical means to explicate and communicate what Henry Mitchell calls 'Black beliefs'. We know that our religious experience affirms the unity and wholeness of life. We need the proper epistemological tools to enable us to release the riches of our religious heritage. The Platonic-Aristotelian logical and metaphysical tradition is alien to this Black religious tradition. The biblical faith has a real affinity with it. But beyond this we need to plunge into the psychology of speech, into our use of symbol, myth, metaphor. We need to discover 'reasons of the heart' and break through to a both/and way of thinking instead of the either/or approach of western thought. Perception rather than conception, intuition rather than reason seems to govern our cognitive processes. I have this in mind in the way I assert liberation *and* reconciliation rather than liberation *or* reconciliation in my programme. We need a frame of reference outside of western thought—structures to both criticise it and correct its deficiencies. As those who have cultural roots in the African setting, we more than Feminist theologians and Liberation theologians may be able to unearth this rich find. This is a team task and it is cross-disciplinary. 'The work is great, the labourers are few, pray that the Lord of the harvest will send more labourers into his vineyard.'

Notes

1. *The Souls of Black Folk* (Greenwich, Connecticut 1968) pp. 104-151.

2. 'Black Theological Ethics: A Bibliographical Essay' in *Journal of Religious Ethics* (1 March 1975) 73-83.

3. 'Perspectives for a Study of Afro-American Religion in the United States' *History of Religions* (1 February, August) 54-65 and 'Structural Similarities'.

4. *Black Sects and Cults* (New York 1972) Ch. 1.

5. 'Same God' in *Book of Negro Folklore* ed. L. Hughes and Arna Bontemps (New York 1958) 228.

6. 'Folklore and Religion' *The Journal of Religious Thought* (26/2, Summer 1970) 5-15.

7. *The Ideological Origins of Black Nationalism* (Boston 1972).

8. *The Ideology of Blackness* (Lexington, Mass. 1971).

PART II

Reports from Local Churches

Chukwudum Barnabas Okolo

Church and Racism:
Nigerian Perspective
(A Report from an African Country)

IN HIS total war against injustice and violation of human rights in Africa, the African has repeatedly turned his attention to white racism and domination. The independent African states which are members of OAU (Organisation of African Unity) for example, have met several times since the organisation was formed in 1963 to condemn particularly racial discrimination in South Africa and to propose measures against an unwanted infringement of human rights and the debasement of man by man. In their opposition to the racist regimes in South Africa and throughout the world, these member states of OAU have displayed a high degree of unity, with a Liberation Committee to aid various liberation movements in southern Africa.

With the OAU as the political organ of condemnation against white racism as an institution, many countries in Black Africa have equally denounced racism in words and actions. It is known, for instance, that Nigeria (and other Black African countries) boycotted the Olympic Games in Montreal, Canada, in 1976. While formerly receiving the Nigerian Contingent back from the Games, one of the Nigerian daily journals gave as the reason for the withdrawal of the athletes, that 'The Federal Military Government will not compromise its stand on the principle of equality and respect for all human beings, irrespective of race or colour'. Indeed, 'for too long has Africa received all sorts of insult from the so-called developed world. For too long has our continent condoned foreign interference and often spiteful behaviour towards us', the paper articulated in no uncertain terms.

But white racism as an institutionalised oppressive system against the Black man in Africa and throughout the world is by no means the concern of the politicians exclusively. The Church, too, has remained a foremost crusader against it and other forms of man's inhumanity to man in the continent. It is the burden of this short paper, 'A Report from an African Country', to show that the Nigerian Church, as many other local churches in Africa, has been equally aware of and concerned about racism as the foremost problem to the Black man in his effort to actualise his full potentials in Africa. It must be admitted, however, that the local churches, including Nigerian, have not put out any explicit programme of action against white racism in the apartheid regime, for

45

instance, but their mood of defiance and protest against it has remained firm and unconditional.

1. NIGERIAN CHURCH AND RACISM

If we define 'racism' with Gerald Leinwand as 'a virulent form of prejudice' (and he defines 'prejudice' as 'the detrimental, preconceived judgment of individuals or groups on the basis of their skin colour, culture, speech patterns, mode of dress, or whatever'),[1] then white racism or the white man's virulent prejudice against the Black man, is by no means a distant, theoretical problem. The Nigerian Church as well as the State is fully and sadly aware of its concrete effects on the Black African throughout his history. Some of these effects in their social and political consequences have been discrimination, segregation, economic exploitation, denial of equal opportunities, disenfranchisement, etc. The Black African in South Africa particularly is no stranger to these evils. Consequently the Nigerian Church in solidarity with the oppressed and discriminated members of the African family has repeatedly condemned racism, which along with other evils continues to diminish the full worth and dignity of the African person and has remained an obstacle to him in playing an active role in his own destiny.

In their joint-condemnation of 'discrimination' on the basis of race or colour, the Catholic Bishops of Nigeria reminded the people of some of the theological reasons for fighting against it and for upholding man's basic rights: 'All members of mankind', they note, 'share the same basic rights and duties as well as the same supernatural destiny: Within a country which belongs to each one, all should be equal before the law, find equal admittance to economic, cultural, civic and social life and benefit from a fair sharing of the nation's riches. The Church therefore condemns all forms of discrimination on the basis of race, religion, etc.'.[2]

Also in their joint pastoral letter, *The Holy Year Jubilee 1975*, the Catholic hierarchy of Nigeria makes a note of the great alienation among men due to their 'egoistic tendencies' and 'instinct of self-aggrandisement'. 'The results for man have been pathetic: warfare, bloodshed, racial discrimination, apartheid, tribalism, to mention a few.' There is at all no doubt that the Church in Nigeria, like the State, is fully aware of the white man's racial burden in the African continent.

This realisation that white racism is the basic problem in Black Africa does not stem solely from the tragic happenings in South Africa and Namibia but from the personal experiences of the Nigerian priests, sisters, and Christian students in American and European countries, among others. The quest for education and the need to build up the Church have made many priests and religious from Nigeria travel to various US and British cities, for example. Their encounter with racism in its overt and covert manifestations, even in churches, has been soul-shattering. 'I never knew I was Black until I reached US', a Nigerian priest once remarked. For it sooner or later dawned on him that the colour of his skin was a liability in his new environment. The Black students in these white nations are generally disappointed and hurt when they realise that their skin colour makes all the difference with regard to the neighbourhood they like to live in, the types of jobs open to them, sometimes, the sort of schools they attend, and friends they are likely to make, and so on. The point is that whether in his own African continent or abroad in the white man's world, the Black African has become fully convinced that white racism is an evil force, that it frustrates him in his struggle to master and control his destiny. The African Church, fully sensitive to the griefs and sorrows of the masses, easily condemns whatever stands in their way as free agents in a free world.

Consequently white racism stands condemned by the Church as well as the State in Africa.

2. BEYOND WHITE RACISM

We must, however, mention that the concern of the Nigerian Church in its protest and solidarity with the oppressed peoples of Africa is definitely beyond racism. Its public protests and condemnations are directed to the more basic problems which confront the African, namely, those social structures: economic, political, educational, etc., which reduce the African to a marginal role in his continent and in the world. The Nigerian Church and all other local churches in Africa collectively decry against colonialism, imperialism, economic exploitation, violence and racism and the economic and political systems that give rise to these evils of human degradation. Unjust social structures are the central concern of all the churches in Black Africa. The 'All Africa Conference of Churches' which met in Kinshasa (Zaïre) in October 1971 made mention of some of the basic problems of the African peoples, 'those tormented by poverty, racism, tribalism, economic, political and elitist exploitation'.

The point we wish to emphasise here is that white racism is but one incidental dimension of oppression against which the total struggle should be directed. It does not at all mean that the attention to be given to racism in Black Africa should be secondary or that it is a secondary factor. Of course racial prejudice is a real problem and should be taken seriously. Neither the fact nor the evilness of it is in dispute. The problem is to recognise its basis and underlying cause. This is located in the economic and political structures themselves. 'There is no doubt that the colour question in South African politics was originally introduced for economic reasons', Steve Biko of South Africa once remarked on the genesis of the Black man's predicament in that part of the world. Julius Nyerere of Tanzania also acknowledged the more basic form of injustice in the modern world particularly with regard to the Third World countries in the address he delivered to a congress of Maryknoll Sisters in New York in 1970.

Like Biko, Nyerere was much more concerned about the broader and much deeper problem than racism, namely, structural oppression at economic, political, social and cultural levels, of which discrimination, segregation, poverty, exploitation, etc., are merely its effects, the tip of the iceberg, so to speak. Consequently neither in the USA nor in South Africa is white racism an end in itself. Its origin, basis, and development are due mainly to its relationship to the economic interests of the white man.

CONCLUSION

Our brief account of 'Church and Racism' in the African continent shows clearly that the Nigerian Church like all other local churches in Africa remains keenly aware of the problem of white racism in Africa. It sees it as more than racial prejudice. Its broad basis is often spelt out as imperialism, neo-colonialism and structural violence. What remains for the Nigerian Church and all other local churches in Africa is *action*, to pass from sterile denunciations and condemnations to concrete actions to change the structures of exploitation themselves. It is simply not enough for the Church to articulate African problems in so many sentimental ways. Actions for a new African society, more humane, more equitable are imperative. Consequently, it is the prime duty of the African Christians and the Church generally to be, in Segundo's phrase, 'artisans of a new Humanity', to be whole-heartedly committed to radical societal changes in the

African continent. This would certainly be a true sign of coming of age for the African Church.

Notes

1. Gerald Leinwand (ed.) *Racism* (New York 1972) p. 15.
2. *The Church and Nigerian Social Problems* (Lagos: Catholic Secretariat 1972) pp. 19-20.

Mariasusai Dhavamony

A Report from India:
The Caste System

1. THE CASTE SYSTEM IN TODAY'S INDIA

ONE OF the most talked about and least understood elements of Indian society is its caste system. Here we are not concerned with the historical origins of the caste system nor with its merits and demerits in the traditional society in India but with the status of caste as a phenomenon in the Indian society today and with its implications.[1] First, caste cannot be identified with class, for in every caste we find educated and uneducated, rich and poor, more powerful and less powerful. Though most members of the upper class belong to the upper castes, there is no necessary correlation between the two. Second, colour is no more a mark of caste, for a brahmin may be utter black and an untouchable may be fair-coloured. Though most upper caste people are fairer than the lower caste, and fairness is aesthetically much valued in women, one cannot tell caste from colour of the skin. The whites as foreigners are considered untouchables. Third, caste is not based on the division between Aryan and non-Aryan, the conqueror and the conquered. Both races are mixed so completely all over India that it is difficult to distinguish Aryans from non-Aryans. Tribal chieftains have become warrior caste, and in the South the Reddis and Nairs, its ruling castes, are not even twice-born. Finally, caste cannot be identified with occupation; for though traditionally many occupations of artisans are of particular castes, the main occupation, agriculture, is open to all, and many castes have non-brahmins as priests. Soldiers come from different castes; one need not be a Bania to be a trader, though many traders are in fact Banias. As we see, the present caste system does not bear much relation to the ancient four *varṇas*: the *brahmin* (priest), the *kshtriya* (warrior), the *Vaishya* (cultivator) and the *shudras* (servant). The untouchables form a group that is outside of these four divisions. Today, the brahmins exist, but it is very difficult to know who is a *kshtriya* or *Vaishya*. The simplest definition of caste is a group of families whose members can marry with each other and can eat in each other's company without believing themselves polluted, and each of these groups has its place in a hierarchy, either above or below or equal to every one of the others; in theory at least everybody knows where each group stands with respect to others. Under the castes there are many sub-castes which are more basic units and which, while clearly part of a larger unit, have enough properties in common, inter-marriage for example, to be a caste-like unit. Marriage and funeral customs, the particular gods of worship may differ

49

from caste to caste. The whole feel and atmosphere of life in one caste is different from that of another. In a society of custom and ritual 'codes of conduct' cover everything and govern how one lives one's life. The idea of pollution gives meaning and motivation in keeping caste rules. It is the fear of pollution which provides sanction for much of what one does or does not do and limits one's contacts outside one's caste.

Untouchability differs in degree rather than in kind from other caste restrictions. In the case of the untouchables marriage and diet restrictions are extended. Not only does one not take water from them, they may not even take water from the same well. Not only does one not marry them, they may not even enter the temple or the house or stroll on the main village streets. Even their cattle may often not drink from the same pool as a brahmin's. Among the untouchables themselves there is untouchability.

Caste is a way of life which keeps a group well knit together by its own customs and ritual, especially by endogamy; hence caste groups exercise great power over their members and are great forces of survival. To break caste is to cut oneself off without any hope of being adopted by another group. Thus the ostracised brahmin cannot become a warrior or even an untouchable since one has to be born within one's caste; only if he finds others of his own caste similarly ostracised can he once more belong to a group because a new sub-caste has been created. The caste system cannot be explained as racism for although the individual is born heir to his caste, his identification with it is assumed to be based upon some sort of psychological and moral heritage which does not go back to any fundamental somatic determinant. The polarity between brahmins and untouchables should help us to understand how distant this case is from racism. The notion of interior purity has been already encountered in the *Shatras*. The purity which the higher castes such as brahmins are supposed to possess is that which is acquired by generations of pure conduct, which consists of doing actions that are pure, eating pure food, by increasing one's own personal sacredness, by the study of the Vedas, and by marriage only with people who have kept pure conduct.[2] It is not the idea of race that governs separation; rather it is the idea of separation, purity, which governs among other things the separation which is elsewhere distinguished as 'race'.[3]

Caste patterns are changing. Mrs Wiser recounts: 'There are fewer caste restrictions than there used to be. Now we young men can do most things together without considering our caste. . . . Just two caste conventions remain which separate us. We do not yet feel free to accept food from someone belonging to a caste lower than our own, and we do not consider marrying anyone outside our own caste. . . . These two rules regarding food and marriage have not interfered with our personal relationships with each other. . . . Friendship is more important than caste, anyhow. . . .'[4]

2. THE INDIAN DEMOCRACY

There has been nothing the Indian democracy has been keener on than equality, economic and social. Economic equality is being realised gradually through land reforms and a crippling system of taxation. Nehru had been very active to achieve economic and social equality. He wrote: 'In India at any rate we must aim at equality. That does not and cannot mean that everybody is physically or intellectually or spiritually equal or can be made so. But it does mean equal opportunities for all and no political, economic or social barrier in the way of any individual or group. . . . It (caste) was an aristocratic approach based on traditionalism. This outlook has to change completely for it is wholly opposed to modern conditions and the democratic ideal.'[5]

The Indian government has pledged to work for social equality; so the untouchables whom Gandhi called Harijans (the children of God) came very high on its plan. There are some 70 million untouchables in India. They have now been given access by law to all public places; any obstruction of them is a criminal offence. The Government has done much to abolish untouchability but it does not signify that untouchables have achieved full equality everywhere in India. They get special electoral weightage through reserved seats; they get preference for government jobs, government lands, for admission to schools and colleges. Grants, loans, scholarships, housing schemes have all been mobilised in the fight against untouchability. Education, urbanisation and industrialisation are the shears with which to cut through the prejudice of millennia.

Among the praiseworthy points of the Indian Constitution is the abolition of the practice of untouchability in any form. Article 17 provides that untouchability is abolished and its practice in any form is forbidden. The enforcement of any disability arising out of untouchability shall be an offence punishable in accordance with law. The act provides that whoever on the ground of untouchability prevents any person from entering into a place of worship which is open to other persons professing the same religion or belonging to the same religious denomination shall be punishable with imprisonment which may extend to six months or with a fine which may extend to Rs 500 or with both.[6]

3. HINDUISM AND CASTE

Gandhi and other leading Hindus hold that caste has nothing to do with religion in general or Hinduism in particular; it is a blot on Hinduism when it has sanctioned it. He says: 'Hinduism has sinned in giving sanction to untouchability. It has degraded us, made us the pariahs of the Empire (British). . . . What crimes for which we condemn the Government (British) as satanic, have not we been guilty of towards our untouchable brethren? . . . Swaraj (self-rule) means that not a single Hindu or Moslem shall for a moment arrogantly think that he can crush with impunity meek Hindus or Moslems. Unless this condition is fulfilled we will gain Swaraj, only to lose it the next moment. We are no better than the brutes until we have purged ourselves of the sins we have committed against our weaker brethren.'[7]

Gandhi believed in the *varṇāśrama dharma* (the law of classes) in the sense that it had in the Vedic period when it was not a rigid caste system but a social organisation based on the division of labour. There should be no distinction of caste or class in the sense of regarding some people as higher than, superior to, others on account of their birth or occupation. But the variety of *varṇas* (classes) based on inherited aptitudes will continue, because it is derived from the healthy principle of division of labour.[8] He interprets the Vedas thus: 'It is the spirit that giveth the light. And the spirit of the Vedas is purity, truth, innocence, chastity, simplicity, forgiveness, godliness and all that makes a man or woman noble and brave. There is neither nobility nor bravery in treating the great and uncomplaining scavengers of the nation as worse than dogs to be despised and spat upon. Would that God gave us the strength and the wisdom to become voluntary scavengers of the nation as the 'suppressed' classes are forced to be.[9]

4. THE CATHOLIC CHURCH AND THE CASTE SYSTEM

In the study of the social doctrine of the Church the first and most important element is man, the human person. Man possesses human nature created by God for a supernatural destiny; as such he enjoys certain duties and rights that are sacred and inalienable, of which none, not even the State, can deprive him. Any social or political system which denies or belittles the high dignity of individual person would tend to destroy the very foundation of social life and organisation. At the same time we should never forget that an individual is essentially a social being. The idea of the dignity of the human person runs like a thread throughout the whole of *Mater et Magistra*.[10] The whole teaching of the Church rests on one basic principle: individual human beings are the foundation, the cause and the end of every social institution. This principle is of universal application, for it takes human nature itself into account, and the varying conditions in which man's life is lived, including the principal characteristics of contemporary society. Justice is to be observed not only in the distribution of wealth but also with regard to the conditions in which men are engaged in producing this wealth. Every man has of his very nature, a need to express himself in his work and thereby to perfect his own being.[11] John XIII said: 'Any human society, if it is to be well ordered and productive, must lay down as a foundation this principle, namely, that every human being is a person, that is, his nature is endowed with intelligence and free will. By virtue of this, he has rights and duties of his own, flowing directly and simultaneously from his very nature, which are therefore universal, inviolable and inalienable.'[12]

A Catholic cannot feel quite relieved when he observes the tenets and tendencies of the Hindu caste system regarding the human dignity, equality, and individual rights. Although it is true that the long-standing caste system has been abolished by the Indian Constitution as opposed to the fundamental rights of the equality of citizens, the Church is well aware that the spirit of the caste did not disappear altogether by mere approval of the Constitution. It is profoundly conscious that the caste spirit persists and it is interfering with the orderly and dignified working of the administration of the country and the functioning of our social institutions, starting from the family and going up to trade unions and the Parliament itself.[13] The Church is besides keenly aware that Christians themselves are affected by it in varying degrees. Goans, Catholics for 400 years, were still twenty years ago looking for brides and bridegrooms of their preconversion castes for their children. Some South Indian churches have made their ex-untouchables sit apart from high caste people.

The Catholic Church has dealt with the problem of caste in various ways. In some areas there was no recognition of caste in the Church, though the non-Christians regarded all Christians together as belonging to a low caste of its own. In South India differences of social status and habits were recognised more or less openly. Thus at Tiruchirapalli we find St Mary's Tope, a colony of Catholic brahmins, founded in 1895, where Christian families may live and keep up their former social customs; and on the west coast the fisher Christians and the Catholic Syrians continued to be quite distinct social groups. Except for the Christians of the South where caste distinctions still persist to some extent, the rest of Indian converts ordinarily disregard them, as these latter Catholics are almost wholly Anglo-Indian or converts from low caste or aboriginals. In general the Catholic Church has abstained from attacking the caste system directly, and has tended to allow it as a lesser evil, though by its teaching it has tried to eliminate the caste spirit and has condemned its extreme manifestations. In so far as the caste system contains certain characteristics which are opposed to Christian doctrine and morals it endeavours to eliminate it first internally by the strength of the Church's positive teaching and practice, so that in time these gradually disappear also externally.

The Indian Government seeks through subsidies to help members of the untouchables to improve their lot in life. Unfortunately, narrow-minded persons sought to exclude from such State aid those untouchables who have become Christians. Thanks to vigorous protests by Catholics and others, many Christian converts have begun to receive the State benefits to which they are entitled by reason of their social background. Christianity's progress among untouchables is bitterly resented, however, by bigoted Hindus. The anti-missionary inquiry committees of Madhya Pradesh and Bharat Pradesh sought to discredit the work of the Christian missions among India's untouchables.[14] But the Church goes on in its work of evangelisation to the poor, the downtrodden and the untouchables, with hope and trust in Jesus Christ.

Notes

1. See Taya Zinkin *Caste today* (Oxford) pp. 1-10 (no year).

2. S. V. Ketkar *The History of Caste in India* Part I (Ithaka, N.Y., 1909) p. 120n.

3. Louis Dumont *Homo Hierarchicus* (London 1972) p. 295.

4. William and Charlotte Wiser *Behind Mud Walls 1930-60* (Berkeley 1971) pp. 225-226.

5. J. Nehru *The Discovery of India* (New York 1946) p. 635.

6. See V. D. Mahajan *Constitutional History of India* Ch. XVI, Delhi 1960.

7. M. Gandhi *Young India* 13-14 September 1921.

8. M. Gandhi *Young India*, 23 April 1945. He writes in the same review: 'I regard *varṇāśrama* as a healthy division of work based on birth. The present ideas of caste are a perversion of the original. There is no question with me of superiority or inferiority. It is purely a question of duty.'

9. M. Gandhi *Young India* 19 January 1921.

10. Encyclical of Pope John XXIII.

11. *Ibid.* nn. 82-94.

12. Pope John XXIII *Pacem in terris* Part I.

13. Father Victor OCD *Social Pastoral Orientation in India* (Allahabad 1966) pp. 57ff.

14. Thomas Pothacamury *The Church in Independent India* (Maryknoll Publication n. 22, New York) p. 21.

Enrique Dussel

A Report on the Situation in Latin America

I PROPOSE to deal here with racism as discrimination against the African slaves, not against the native Indians.[1] A brief remark first about some of the postulates used. There is a school of 'economicism' which would see class economic domination as the sole cause of racism (assessment *a* in the diagram below). On the other hand, there exists a 'subjectivist psychologism' which denies any possibility of considering the problem if one has not first suffered humiliation 'in one's own skin' (assessment *b*). Then there is the classic 'biological racism' which seeks to define the cause of racism as the natural or physical differences between individuals of different races, with the supposition that one race is genetically superior to another (assessment *c*). Finally, there are those who adopt a 'cultural' viewpoint and see everything being played out on the level of symbols, in cultural traditions, dance and song (assessment *d*). In fact the problem of racist domination operates on all these levels, once one understands that its chief characteristic is a part of *ideological* development.

Diagram 1

The 'practical circle' of racist ideology

```
                        'Class' economic and
                        political assessment
                                 a
                                 ↓
Assessment from physical or           'Racist'          Cultural or symbolic
biological difference       c →       ideology    ← d   evaluation
                                 ↑
                                 b
                        Psychological interpretation
                        of domination
```

The struggle against racist domination therefore needs to take account of all these levels. A theology of liberation of the Black population of Latin America should also take account of all the different assessments if it is not to be left working from a partial standpoint.

1. HISTORICAL CLASS ASSESSMENT[2]

The Portuguese discovery of the route to India in the fifteenth century and the conquest of America by the Spaniards and Portuguese led to the decline of the Arab commercial world (since that route was no longer the only one open to world trade), and to a crisis in all the kingdoms of the Savannah countries (as a result of Arab decline), mainly because Europe now sought its gold in America.[3] This explains why communities such as the Soninke, Sosso, Mandingas, Sourhay, Haoussa, Bornu, etc., which were divided into ruling and ruled classes, began to engage in the *sale* of their African brothers on the West Coast of Africa, in order to produce a continuing level of commercial profit. The Portuguese, the English, the Dutch and the French all became involved in the dreadful slave trade from Africa to tropical Latin America, which led to an agriculture on the 'plantations' dedicated to the growing of cash crops for export: sugar, cocoa, cotton, etc. And in Latin America a 'slave-based patriarchal Catholicism' appeared.[4]

Although the Spanish crown had banned Jews, Moors, 'new Christians' and *negroes* from going to the West Indies, the latter were already common in Santo Domingo by 1505. The 'sugar cycle', lasting till 1520, started there, and the sugar mills were populated with African slaves. 'All work linked to the land was carried out by African slaves. The slave population of Melchor de Torres reached 900. By 1548 the number of mills and mines had reached thirty-five.'[5]

E. Genovese has proved that the production systems operative in the plantations were not anti-capitalist, though it must be recognised that the English and Dutch slave-owning bourgeoisie in the Caribbean developed a more modern and truly capitalist system than the Spanish—even than the most developed of the Spanish societies, the slave-owning middle-classes in Cuba. 'Slavery should be seen primarily as a *class* question, and only secondarily as a racial question.'[6] Nicolás Sánchez Albornoz points to the same conclusion: 'Negroes were first and foremost capital goods, and their importation was governed by the rules of commerce and the stimulus of trade.'[7] Of course the system was not the same in the case of the patriarchal paternalism of the mill owner of North-East Brazil as in that of the English capitalist who lived in London and owned 'plantations' in Jamaica, Trinidad or Guyana. But the fact is that Latin America had a slave population.

As early as 1513 the Spanish king gave the first licence to charge two ducats for each African slave sold. By 1578 this had risen to thirty ducats. The Africans were treated monstrously, not only by the human hunt in Africa and the inhuman passage across the Atlantic—during which up to 30 per cent died—but equally by the 'palming' (measuring height and therefore price) and branding (with a hot iron on the back, chest or thigh, to show that the tax had been paid) to which they were subjected once they arrived at the ports of Cartagena, Vera Cruz, Bahía, Río, Pernambuco, etc.

Besides the Caribbean and Brazil, the whole of northern South America (Venezuela and Colombia) and the Pacific coast down to Guayaquil had a Black majority. In Mexico, Central America, Peru and the River Plate district, Black slaves were used as domestic servants or *Majordomos* in charge of Indians. Whatever use they were put to, the basic reason for their presence in Latin America was mercantile capitalism.

2. THE ABOLITION OF SLAVERY IN LATIN AMERICA

One factor was the work *Instauranda Aethiopum Salute* written by Alonso de Sandóval, SJ, at the end of the seventeenth century. (He taught St Peter Claver, the apostle of the slaves, in Cartagena.) Another was the formation of slave and negro confraternities in the colonial period. Another the endless revolts by Africans—in Haïti

Table 1

Total importation of slaves to America from the fifteenth to the ninteenth centuries (from Curtin, p. 178). Figures in thousands.

Region or nation	1451-1600	1601-1700	1701-1800	1811-1870	Total
United States	—	—	348·0	51·0	399·0
Latin America	75·0	292·5	578·6	606·0	1,552·1
British Caribbean	—	263·7	1,401·3	—	1,665·0
Jamaica	—	85·1	662·4	—	747·5
Barbados	—	134·5	252·5	—	387·0
Leeward Islands, St Lucia, Tobago, etc.	—	44·1	371·9	—	416·1
Trinidad	—	—	22·4	—	22·4
Grenada	—	—	67·0	—	67·0
Other British West Indies	—	—	25·0	—	25·0
French Caribbean	—	155·8	1,348·4	96·0	1,600·2
Haïti	—	74·6	789·7	—	864·3
Martinique	—	66·5	258·3	41·0	365·8
Gaudelupe	—	12·7	237·1	41·0	290·8
Louisiana	—	—	28·3	—	28·3
French Guyana	—	2·0	35·0	14·0	51·0
Dutch Caribbean	—	40·0	460·0	—	500·0
Danish Caribbean	—	4·0	24·0	—	28·0
Brazil	50·0	560·0	1,891·4	1,145·4	3,646·8
Rest of the World	149·9	25·1	—	—	175·0
Europe	48·8	1·2	—	—	50·0
São Tomé	76·1	23·9	—	—	100·0
Atlantic Isles	25·0	—	—	—	25·0
TOTAL	274·9	1,341·1	6,051·7	1,898·4	9,566·1
Annual quota	1·8	13·4	55·0	31·6	22·8

alone in 1522, 1679 and 1691; in Santo Domingo in 1523, 1537, 1548, etc.; in the British Antilles in 1647, 1674, 1702, 1733 and 1759; few as impressive as the establishment of a real State in the 'shanty-town' of Los Palmares in Brazil, in which the hero Zumbi Gangozuma was killed in 1695. A major factor was the way the Black leader and liberator of Haïti, Toussaint Louverture, showed the world that negroes could be political leaders and rulers. But as a matter of historical fact, the abolition of slavery was chiefly due to the growth of industrial capitalism. While mercantile capitalism needed slaves in order to export tropical products, industrial capitalism needed *free* workers whose labour it could buy for wages. This does not mean that a class-based racism did not carry on in the capitalist system, but industrial capitalism was incompatible with the slavery of the plantations.

So, 'the abolition of the slave trade was declared by the Supreme Court of Caracas in 1810, by Hidalgo in Mexico in the same year, by the Chilean Parliament in 1811 and by the Government in Buenos Aires in 1812'.[8]

For the same reasons that led to the victory of the northern states over the 'old South' of the plantations based on patriarchal slave-owning in the American Civil War, the São Paulo coffee magnates in Brazil (1870-80) destroyed the aristocratic slave owners of the North-East of the country with the law *Lei aurea* of 13 May 1888, which signalled the abolition of slavery and the triumph of the capitalism (though dependent) of the South.

While slavery disappeared from Latin America in the nineteenth century, 'racism' as a *class ideology* discriminating against the manual labourer, the worker, the marginalised Blacks, did not. In Latin American countries with a large Black population, racism is still a living, active, real social injustice.

3. THE BLACK PRESENCE IN LATIN AMERICA

The importance of this question can be seen from the fact that by the end of this century Brazil alone will have a Black and mulatto population of 80 million, making it perhaps the country with the largest negro population in the world. The survival of African customs and religions is everywhere obvious—Bantu, Fanti-ashanti, Black Islam, Calabar and Yoruba with its famous *Orishas*.[9] The most relevant forms of creative expression are the Voodoo of Haïti and the *candomblé* of north-eastern Brazil, with their own spirits, gods, saints, cosmologies, liturgies and dances, ecstasies, ways of life and popular communities. Piling one form of syncretism on another, they show traits of African religions, Catholicism and even Protestantism, together with spiritualism and magic. Athur Ramos defines *macumba*—another African cult in Brazil—as a mixture of *gégé* (Fon), *nago* (Yoruba), *musulmi* (Black Islam), Bantu, *camboclé* (Indian), spiritualism and Catholicism.

All such cults derive from three main traditions: genuine African (survivals such as the Bantu 'sacred dances'); negro folklore originating in the plantations of America (through a process of 'creole-ising', like the stories of 'Papa John' who deceives his master, through which the slaves affirmed their own personalities and laughed at their masters); and finally, the whole sphere of the infiltration of Black culture into the dominant white culture, through symbols, music or effective participation by Blacks in the white way of life.

In recent decades a new political situation for the Blacks in Latin America has begun to emerge. This has happened mainly in the Caribbean, with revolutionary leaders; in

Table 2

The Negro and Mulatto population of Latin America in 1940
(with percentage of the total population of each country)

Country	Negroes	%	Mulattoes	%
Brazil	5,789,924	14·0	8,276,321	20·01
Antilles	5,500,000	39·29	3,000,000	21·43
British Guyana	100,000	29·30	80,000	23·44
Dutch Guyana	17,000	9·55	20,000	11·23
French Guyana	1,000	0·25	1,000	0·25
Belize	15,000	25·55	20,000	34·03
Colombia	405,076	4·5	2,205,382	24·32
Venezuela	100,000	2·79	1,000,000	27·93
Nicaragua	90,000	6·52	40,000	2·88
Honduras	55,272	4·99	10,000	0·90
El Salvador	100	0·0001	100	0·0001
Costa Rica	26,900	4·09	20,000	3·14
Guatemala	4,011	0·12	2,000	0·06
Mexico	80,000	0·41	40,000	2·04
Ecuador	50,000	2·0	150,000	6·0
Peru	29,054	0·41	80,000	0·71
Bolivia	7,800	0·26	5,000	0·15
Paraguay	5,000	0·52	5,000	0·52
Uruguay	10,000	0·46	50,000	2·30
Argentina	5,000	0·038	10,000	0·076
Chile	1,000	0·02	3,000	0·06

the Mosquitia region of Nicaragua, and even through the presence of Cuban negro soldiers in wars of liberation in Africa itself. Could the Africans who left those shores as slaves in the past produce today the liberators of their brothers in their continent of origin? History has long and mysterious ways which must be explored and deciphered.

As can be seen, the negro population is concentrated in tropical produce regions, the old 'plantations': the Brazilian coastal region, the Caribbean and the Pacific coast from southern Paraguay to Ecuador.

4. RACISM AND LIBERATION THEOLOGY IN LATIN AMERICA

The question of racism poses a challenge to liberation theology in its growth process. Domination of one *nation* by another (understood through the theory of dependence), of one *class* by another (where sociological considerations and those of political economy are at stake), of one *sex* by another (where Freudian categories must be taken into account), is not of the same order as domination of one *race* by another, which involves a multi-level complex of economic, political, psychological, cultural and symbolic, ideological and other factors. Theology has to deal with liberation from all these dominations epistemologically, taking account of the differences between each. The erotic-subjective factor is one thing, the economic-objective another, the symbolic-cultural yet another. Ideology cannot be set aside, either, but needs to be situated on the level of its relative autonomy and so assessed in relation to the other factors.

I have said that industrial capitalism was the basic cause of the freeing of the slaves in the plantation system. Yet German national capitalism (the Krupps and Thyssens, who are never mentioned nowadays but who were responsible for Hitler) has in our century been the economic and political starting-point for anti-Jewish racist ideology. So capitalism is at one time anti-slavery and at another anti-Jewish racist (in order to eliminate international Jewish capital from Germany). In relation to the negroes, capitalism uses colour difference as an ideological tool in the domination of the middle class over the working class—the urban proletariat, since in Latin America the negroes are rarely peasants.

The theological *sin* of racism takes on connotations of economic and political domination, psychological domination (the sadistic aggressiveness of the dominator, the masochistic passivity of the dominated), symbolic domination (the devil is Black, like sin), and ideological domination as such (the negro race is inferior). This is why Boesak's 'the courage to be'[10] is immensely important. Not only as negation of the negation involved in oppression, but also as affirmation of Black, African actuality, the dignity of being a *historic people* with its own traditions, heroes, art and religion.

All this has to be linked *explicitly* to the question of the *oppressed class* in Latin America's system of dependent capitalism. The Black struggle for liberation is a struggle for the affirmation of *negritude* within a national project of liberation, together with other oppressed races, and aiming at a socialist system for Latin America. Without this strategic socio-political focus, liberation of the race can become an absolute, a 'reformism', leading in the end to a dissolution of its efforts and an attack on the wrong enemies. These are not 'whites' as such but the whites who dominate the capitalist system. To regard any white as an enemy for the simple fact of being white is to fail to distinguish which whites use racism for their own advantage, and, at the same time to alienate white allies who are also *oppressed* by those who dominate both white and black. Theology cannot bypass such questions: if it does, it could become populist or reformist and cease to be liberation theology properly so-called.[11]

Translated by Paul Burns

Notes

1. I have given a partial treatment of this question in 'Modern Christianity in the face of "the other"' in *Concilium* 130 (10/1979) 49.

2. The following is a classified bibliography of the question:

(i) *Latin America in general:*

J. Saco *Historia de la esclavitud de la raza negra en el Nuevo Mundo* (Havana 1938); E. Vila Vilar *Hispanoamérica y el comercio de esclavos* (Seville 1977); R. Mellafe *Breve historia de la esclavitud negra en América Latina* (Mexico 1973); L. Rout *The African Experience in Spanish America: 1502 to the Present* (Cambridge 1976); F. Knight *The African Dimension in Latin American Societies* (New York 1974); L. Fonor *Slavery in the New World* (Englewood Cliffs 1969); J. Gratus 'The Great White Lie: slavery, emancipation and changing racial attitudes' in *Monthly Review* (New York 1973).

(ii) *Particular areas*

(*a*) Brazil:

F. Cardoso *Capitalismo e escravidão no Brasil meridional* (São Paulo 1977); R. Conrad *The Destruction of Brazilian Slavery* (Berkeley 1972); P. Verger *Flux et reflux de la traite des nègres entre le golfe de Bénin et Bahía de Todos os Santos* (Paris 1968).

(*b*) The Caribbean:

J. Handler *The Unappropriated People: Freedmen in the Slave Society of Barbados* (Baltimore 1974); H. Aimes *A History of Slavery in Cuba: 1511-1968* (New York 1970); V. J. Baptiste *Haïti: sa lutte pour l'émancipation* (Paris 1957); O. Patterson *The Sociology of Slavery in Jamaica* (Jamaica 1973); L. Díaz Soler *La esclavitud negra en Puerto Rico* (San Juan 1957); G. Martin *Histoire de l'esclavage dans les colonies françaises* (Paris 1948); J. Fouchard *Les Marrons de la liberté* (Paris 1972).

(*c*) Mexico:

G. Aguirre *La población negra de México 1519-1910* (Mexico 1946); R. Brady *The Emergence of a Negro Class in Mexico 1524-1640* (Iowa 1965).

(*d*) Central America:

W. Sherman *Forced Native Labor in XVI-century Central America* (London 1979); S. Zavala *Contribución a la historia de las instituciones coloniales de Guatemala* (Guatemala 1953); L. Diez Castillo *Los cimarrones y la esclavitud en Panamá* (Panama 1968).

(*e*) Colombia and Venezuela:

A. Escalante *El negro en Colombia* (Bogotá 1968); J. Palacios *La trata de negros por Cartagena 1650-1750* (Tunja 1973); M. Acosta *Vida de los esclavos negros en Venezuela* (Caracas 1966); E. Tronconis *Documentos para el estudio de los esclavos negros en Venezuela* (Caracas 1969).

(*f*) The Southern Tip:

R. E. Chace *The African Impact on Colonial Argentina* (Santa Barbara 1969); C. Sempat *El tráfico de esclavos en Córdoba 1588-1610* (Córdoba 1965); E. Scheuss de Studer *La trata de negros en el Río de la Plata en el siglo XVIII* (Buenos Aires 1958); G Cruz *La abolición de la esclavitud en Chile* (Santiago 1942); C. Rama *Los agro-uruguayos* (Montevideo 1967).

(*g*) Peru:

F. Bowser *The African Slave in Colonial Peru 1524-1650* (Stamford 1974).

3. See F. Braudel 'De l'or du Soudan à l'argent d'amérique' in *Annales E.S.C.* (Paris[1] 1946) 1-22.

4. See G. Freyre *Casa grande e senzala* (Rio[18] 1979).

5. F. Moya Pons *Historia Colonial de Santo Domingo* (Santo Domingo 1974) p. 71ff.

6. See E. Genovese *Esclavitud y capitalismo* (Barcelona 1971).

7. *La problación en América latina* (Madrid 1973) p. 93; see P. Curtin *The Atlantic Slave Trade* (Madison 1975).

8. R. Mellafe in the work cited in note 2, pp. 141ff; see E. E. Williams *Capitalism and Slavery* (New York 1944).

9. See R. Bastide *Las Américas negras* (Madrid 1967) pp. 121-207.

10. See A. Boesak *Farewell to Innocence* (New York 1977).

11. These questions were discussed at a seminar held in Kingston, Jamaica in December 1979.

Virgil Elizondo

A Report on Racism:
A Mexican American in the
United States[1]

OF THE 14·6 million persons listing themselves as being of 'Spanish origin' in our nation, the majority are 'Mexican American', a term which identifies the people of the United States of America who are of Mexican descent. Politically they are citizens of the US—many by birth and others through naturalisation. There are an additional four to six million Mexican people living in the United States without legal status or documentation. Culturally and linguistically the people are Mexican. Racially, the group is a mixture of European and native American, that is, they are a *mestizo* people. Many of the people have emigrated to the United States of America, but a significant number were already living where they live today when the United States of America expanded its borders after the war with Mexico. In 1848, about 50 per cent of the Mexican territory became a part of the USA; subsequently the Mexican people of the South-West United States became a conquered people—foreigners in their own homeland.

The Mexican American is the largest of various Hispanic groups living in the United States. The other groups are Puerto Ricans (who were assumed into the political boundaries of the United States in the 1890s), the Cubans and smaller numbers from all the other countries of Latin America. The presence of the Hispanic in the United States is annually increasing because of on-going migrations and because the Hispanic still likes to have larger families than those of the mainline USA.

1. THE PAST

The hatred and disdain which the Mexican Americans and other Hispanics have experienced in the United States can only be appreciated within the over-all context of 'Americanism'. 'Americanism' is the fundamental religion and culture of 'The American Way of Life'. From the very beginning, the first Northern European immigrants to North America saw themselves as the New Israel. They believed they were elected by God for a special destiny and a special role in the formation of the kingdom of God on earth. This sense of divine election and, therefore, of divinely established superiority over all other peoples—Catholics, Latin Europeans, Africans, Asiatics and the natives of the American continent—was present from the very beginning. This sense of divine election has become one of the deepest collective traits of the white Anglo-Saxon Protestant English-speaking people of the United States, otherwise known as the WASP. The early preaching of that time brings out clearly the identification of the US experience with 'Providence', 'God's special election' and the 'New Israel'. Thus the nation-building enterprise becomes a deeply religious experience. Even to this day, nationalism has functioned as the fundamental religion of the United States. The various confessional groups will maintain their own particular creeds and practice, but they will be reinterpreted and lived through the values, attitudes and prejudices of the new nation. It must be pointed out that this nationalism was deeply anti-Catholic and racist in nature. The United States began after the Protestant splits in Europe and the majority of the early settlers were escaping the various forms of religious tyranny in Europe. Rome was considered by them to be the main obstacle to religious freedom and human dignity. Racially, they were convinced of their own supremacy over all the others. This religious racial conviction was supported and promulgated by the philosophical theories and the religious preaching of that time. In 1844 Robert Baird, considered the first major American Church historian, wrote: 'In a word, our national character is that of the Anglo-Saxon race . . . and men must study Saxon institutions, and Saxon laws and usages . . . for the Germanic or Teutonic are the chief supports of the ideas and institutions of evangelical Christianity and hold in their hands the theoretical and practical mission of Protestantism for the world.'[2]

In the United States, religious educational, economic, political and communications institutions have all worked together to confirm and reinforce the conviction that white, Anglo-America was indeed God's chosen vessel—a superior people destined by Divine Providence to rule over all the lesser peoples of the world.

Armed with this mentality, the United States set out to expand its borders to the rest of the Americas. This expansionist movement took on the nature and fervour of an evangelical crusade. In the 1800s, many people from the United States started to migrate west into Mexican territory. Some went into Mexico legally at the invitation of the Mexican government and many more moved illegally into the Mexican territories with total disregard for Mexican laws and customs. All were convinced of being agents of God's manifest destiny. It must be noted clearly that from the very first contacts, the superiority-minded North Americans looked upon the Mexicans with great disdain. The Mexicans were generally brown-skinned, *mestizo*, Roman Catholic and Spanish-speaking. To the Protestant, racially 'pure' Anglo-Americans, the Mexicans appeared as degenerate and damned! The Mexican was the very opposite of everything the United States considered as normative for humanity and basic for divine election. The Mexican appeared as the absolute contradiction of the WASP model of human existence.

Since the beginning of the Anglo-American conquest, the Mexicans have been systematically insulted, dehumanised, exploited, segregated, abused, oppressed and massacred. Lynchings and murders of Mexicans have been the accepted order of the day from the very first contacts in the early 1800s, even to our day.[3] All the institutions, including the United States churches, have worked together to systematically discredit and destroy anything Mexican. Popular literature has continually portrayed the Mexican as a lazy, drunken, dumb, good-for-nothing, subhuman race. The churches have strengthened this negative view by looking upon the faith expressions of the people as uninformed, superstitious and childish. We have been deprived of a clergy and an episcopacy of our own and have been spoken to by Church leaders, but never dialogued with. Church laws have been imposed upon the people but the gospel has seldom, if ever, been presented to them. Juridical institutions have conspired to use justice in favour of the 'conquistadores' from the North and against the conquered inhabitants.

Educational institutions have either ignored the Mexican American or have helped our people to 'drop out' of school. Books, novels, movies and TV have consistently portrayed the Mexican as vicious bandits, lazy peasants or humorous buffoons.[4] Economic institutions have exploited the Mexican American workers and political institutions have kept the people from participation. An abundant supply of uneducated and foreign-speaking workers have been much more profitable to the large rancher and agricultural economy of the United States than a slave force. The poor Mexican worker took the place of the slaves when the slaves became too expensive to maintain. The sweat, broken backs and lives of the exploited Mexican workers have been the life-source of much of the wealth of this country. Yet the very powers which have exploited the people and become rich through their work, have discredited them as lazy, unreliable and irresponsible.

2. THE PRESENT

It would be excellent if all this were only history. But the sad story of racism and exploitation continues today in many ways—some quite open and others more subtle and unsuspected.

The migrant and the undocumented worker still continues to be exploited and maligned throughout the country. School districts of heavy Hispanic concentrations continue to be inadequate and below standard. As a result of this, Hispanics are still prevented from participating in higher education programmes and professional schools. Police brutality still continues and frequently goes unpunished. High percentages of Hispanics are underpayed, underemployed and denied advancements into positions of responsibility. The jails are still packed with an unusually high percentage of Blacks and Hispanics. Real estate agents still manage to refuse sale of property to non-wanted Hispanics through various subtle but very effective means. The military forces send high concentrations of Hispanics to the frontline, combat readiness zone of the East-West border of Europe. Hispanics are not welcomed nor accepted in many of the Anglo churches. Cities still exist with racially segregated churches. This litany could easily go on for many pages but space does not permit to enumerate.

3. THE FUTURE

There have been strong movements in the United States to combat racism and to eradicate it from our country. The movements have been civil, educational, economic and religious. Blacks, Browns and Whites have all participated in these efforts. In the 1980s, those of us working in these movements are becoming aware that whereas there is a sincere good-will and conviction on the part of many to stamp out racism, the white WASPish racist mentality is still so deeply ingrained on the mainline consciousness of the people of the United States that it will not be easily eradicated. This is an attitude that cannot be eliminated easily, even though many want to do away with it.

In spite of this, great strides are being made. The United States Catholic Church now has over a dozen Hispanic bishops, although Hispanic leadership is still absent from the religious orders, and from Catholic colleges and universities. Associations such as PADRES, for Hispanic priests, and HERMANAS, for Hispanic religious women, are strong action-oriented groups. The Mexican American Cultural Center in San Antonio is devoted to research, education, formation and publications promoting the positive image and status of the Mexican American and new models of cultural understanding and interchange. In many larger cities such as Los Angeles, San Antonio, Houston and

Chicago, community organisation groups are flourishing. San Antonio, Texas, today is the ninth largest city in the United States and the only city to have both a Mexican American bishop and a Mexican American mayor. Political education groups are helping the people to develop political skills so as to take a responsible role in the affairs of the community. The Fund for Theological Education is actively seeking outstanding Hispanic ministers to finance their ongoing education so that they may become experts in the various fields of Church needs. Even though this group is largely Protestant, it is taking the initiative in helping the Hispanic priests and sisters to continue their doctoral studies.

Progress is starting. But the road ahead is much more difficult and much longer than anyone had suspected a few years back. Much has been accomplished, many barriers have been destroyed, new understanding has been introduced, new structures are beginning to emerge, but much more still needs to be accomplished. In fact, the more that we are able to accomplish, the more we realise how much deeper the questions are and how much more still needs to be done. Basically we are still living in the midst of a white, Anglo-Saxon dominated society wherein anyone who does not meet the racial-cultural-linguistic qualifications will always continue to be foreign, inferior, undesirable and easily exploitable.

Notes

1. Because of the complexity of the topic which I have been asked to address in this brief paper, I will conclude the report with a brief bibliography of other works which treat the subject much more extensively.

2. Marty Martin *The Righteous Empire* (New York 1970) p. 23.

3. Consult Adolfo Acuña *Occupied America* pp. 26-27. Also S. Chamberlain *My Confession* (New York 1956).

4. Allen Woll 'How Hollywood has Portrayed the Hispanics' in *The New York Times* 1 March 1981, pp. 17 and 22.

Bibliography

Acuña, R. *Occupied America—A History of Chicanos* (New York 1981).

Arroyo, A. M. S. *Prophets Denied Honor—An Anthology on the Hispano Church of the United States* (Maryknoll 1980).

Bernard, H. R. and Duran, L. I. *Introduction to Chicano Studies* (New York 1973).

Burma, H. J., ed. *Mexican Americans in the United States. A Reader* (Cambridge, Mass. 1970).

Elizondo, V. *Christianity and Culture* (Huntington, Indiana 1975).

Elizondo, V. *Mestizaje: The Dialectic of Cultural Birth and the Gospel* (San Antonio 1978).

Elizondo, V. 'A Way for the Church to Regard Hispanics' *Origins* 10 No. 13 (1980).

Foley, D., and Mota, C., Post, D., Lozano, I. *From Peons to Politicos: Ethnic Relations in a South Texas Town 1900-1977* (Austin, Texas 1977).

Gamio, M. *Mexican Immigrants to the United States—A Study of Human Migration and Adjustment* (New York 1971).

Hurtado, J. *An Attitudinal Study of Social Distance between the Mexican American and the Church* (San Antonio, Texas 1975).

Marty, M. *The Righteous Empire: The Protestant Experience in America* (New York 1972).

McWilliams, C. *North From Mexico—The Spanish-Speaking People of the United States* (New York 1968).

Meier, M. S. and Rivera, F. *The Chicanos, A History of the Mexican American* (New York 1972).

Morales, A. *Ando Sangrando (I Am Bleeding)—A Study of Mexican American-Police Conflict* (La Puerta, California 1972).

Samora, J. *Los Mojados: The Wetback Story* (Notre Dame, Indiana 1971).

Shockley, J. S. *Chicano Revolt in a Texas Town* (Notre Dame, In. 1974).

Shockley, J. S. 'Brothers and Sisters to Us' US Bishops' Pastoral Letter on Racism in our Day, 14 November 1979.

Shockley, J. S. 'Cultural Pluralism in the United States' A statement by the US Catholic Bishops, 14 April 1980.

Carl Starkloff

The Church, Racism and North American Natives

THE ROOTS of racism grow deep, and they are intricately intertwined with countless sub- and unconscious motivations. Webster defines racism as 'an assumption of inherent racial superiority or the purity and superiority of certain races, and consequent discrimination against other races'. The definition only touches the surface, especially for one who seeks to understand racial attitudes towards Amerindian people. In his prize-winning work, *Friend and Foe*, Cornelius J. Jaenen offers a vivid description, from both sides, of the New World-Old World confrontation in the seventeenth century. Jaenen accepts Francis Parkman's thesis that of all Europeans, the French were the most accepting of native peoples, but that they too fluctuated in their reactions between 'noble savage' and 'depraved barbarian' concepts.[1] The explorers brought with them the most naïve expectations of finding a Golden Age people in America, and then reacted severely when they were disappointed.[2] From Jaenen's description, we might say that the American native was in many respects a preconceived religious experience, either of the angelic or the demonic, in the European imagination.

Attitudes have not changed that much over the four centuries. Europeans still often harbour uncritical assumptions about New World aborigines, and seem eager to embrace every contemporary romantic viewpoint. Euro-Americans who live removed from Indians reflect similar attitudes, while those in close proximity often show the crudest forms of racial hatred based on fear, ignorance and immature and uncritical reaction to the tragic social conditions of so many native tribes. Their racism is reflected in turn through a reverse prejudice among native peoples, and a reactionary tendency to discriminate against whites and even against 'mixed-bloods' in their own tribes. All of these attitudes, at least those of white North Americans, are exaggerations and distortions rooted in limited or no personal acquaintance. As Lee Cook, a brilliant young Catholic layman-activist and Chippewa Indian, once told a leadership group of Native Americans and Church ministers, the real trouble is that no one *knows* any Indians. Personal knowledge would make it clear that Native Americans are not supernatural beings, not generally saints, not demons; they are simply human beings with human virtues and vices. But this murky state of things is the situation with which the Church must deal—and the problem is not outside of but deep within the Church itself.

There is beyond doubt a gross form of racism directed against Amerindian people, based simply on racial features. But this, literally, is a skin-deep explanation. It is my own contention that the conflict is not based so much on physical differences, which have never, for example, prevented extensive intermarriage, but on deeply misunderstood cultural and religious differences. The white American both fears the native people (and thus hopes even at this late hour to tame and 'assimilate' them) and idolises a certain romantic image of them, often showing great resentment when they fail to fulfil expectations.[3]

Vine Deloria has attributed anti-Indian injustice to a far more pragmatic strain in the Euro-American character: 'The problem is and always has been the adjustment of the legal relationship between the Indian tribes and the federal government, between the true owners of the land and the usurpers.'[4] But Deloria also sees how the white American's conviction of racial and cultural inferiority in native peoples makes it a simple matter for them to conclude that Indians need not be given equal justice under the law.[5] It is easy, I believe, to 'bracket out' from our systems of social and economic justice those whose customs, religion and life-style seems peculiar to us.

The official Church's contemporary (and reformed) attitude towards Native American peoples receives its impetus from Vatican Council II, especially its documents on the Church today, the missions, non-Christian religions and religious freedom. Speaking of documents such as these and of the entire Council, Karl Rahner could propose the thesis: '. . . the Second Vatican Council is, in a rudimentary form, still groping for identity, the Church's first official self-actualisation *as* a world Church'.[6] That is, the Church is for the first time recognising its identity far beyond its European cultural boundaries.

Rahner's thesis can be applied with equal validity to the subsequent statements of the American Catholic Bishops dealing with Native Americans, as well as to contemporary efforts to implement their statements. The bishops' 1977 document on American Indians took aim at some of the more significant problems: respect for distinctive traditions of peoples, the relation between cultural and Christian faith, the problems of injustice based on race and culture, and the need for the Church to support native efforts to achieve justice.[7] As far as Indian peoples are concerned, the document published two years later on racism is much less specific, and, while showing a deepening sense of racial justice and of the subtleties involved in racism, is still dealing with the very rudiments of anti-racist theory and praxis. As the document itself wisely states, '. . . we refrain from giving detailed answers to complex questions on which we ourselves have no competence. Instead, we propose several guidelines of a general nature'.[8]

The American Church (with similar efforts in Canada) has indeed begun to search and probe. In March of 1980 an edition of *Catholic Update* discussed racism and means to combat it. Most of the issue simply digests the pastoral letter on racism, but specifies ways to combat this evil: openness to a change of heart, avoidance of xenophobia, elimination of stereotypes, advocacy against racial inequities, examining racial attitudes within the Church, supporting inner-city Catholic schools, backing public policies for racial equality, and keeping alive the dream of a united world.[9] I would like to devote the final portion of this article to matters touching two of these points—'xenophobia' and racial attitudes within the Church.

Shortly after the emergence of the bishops' pastoral letter on American Indians, the United States Catholic Conference began to take steps to implement the more general guidelines of that letter. One of these means was a conference on Native American catechesis, held on the Papago Reservation in Arizona in November of 1978. The conference was an excellent, if small, beginning—a tiny splash whose ripples have continued to spread outward. During the conference one member showed the group a recent catechism on the psalms, purporting to be both pedagogically and racially sensitive in its illustrations of how God protects His children. Two double-page cartoons, intended to portray this divine protection, showed a small child (with Caucasian features) lost in the wilderness and surrounded by his 'enemies'. The enemies, true to good Hollywood tradition, were a horde of Indian warriors lurking in the rocks and trees. With the help of God, the child triumphs, leaving his enemies dead and scattered over the landscape. Of course, the entire assemblage at the conference protested the astounding obtuseness of this work, and the publishers had the text altered eventually. But the incident only serves to highlight a problem lying deep at the roots of Church attitudes, both among the grass roots and among those forming official policy.

The best response (one of a scant few, to my knowledge) to the episcopal letter on Indian people was a brief article by Silvio Fittipaldi of Villanova University. If Fittipaldi's comment had any shortcomings, these probably lay in his failure to acknowledge the immensely complex historical and pastoral problems facing those who attempt cross-cultural dialogue with Native Americans. But the author, both respectfully and perceptively, points out some of the problems contained in the bishops' assertion that 'The Good News' is not bound by time or human structures and is thus able to thrive in any culture.[10] He finds a certain simplistic strain in the pastoral letter, which ignores the possibility and likelihood that those who present the universal gospel also have their cultural biases.[11]

Juan Luis Segundo's excellent little book, *The Hidden Motives of Pastoral Action*, comes to mind here.[12] Segundo calls upon the Church to reflect on its various underlying assumptions and ideologies as it serves oppressed peoples. I believe Fittipaldi's critique of the American bishops' document places the finger upon one very subtle hidden assumption, indeed on a deep half-conscious ideology—namely, that the Good News as European missionaries have proclaimed it is truly the *universal* gospel. This requires careful examination.

It is certainly no simple matter to discover what elements in Church proclamation and doctrine *do* constitute 'essentials', and which are simply cultural trappings. No doubt, too we simply have to acknowledge the profound influence that 'western civilisation' has exercised on Church history, and be prepared to work within that historical framework even as we move forward from it. Yet how many cultural and racial assumptions—even xenophobia!—may lie beneath the Church's laws and requirements about, for example, forms of worship and Church discipline? One of the implications of Rahner's thesis on Vatican II would seem to deal with pastoral praxis in the light of true universality.

The Catholic Churches in the United States and Canada are now engaged in an ever-deepening and widening dialogue with native peoples, and this dialogue includes a number of open-minded and open-hearted bishops. Missionaries and bishops in many areas are seeking to establish greater 'mutuality' between the sending Church and local native communities, respecting the many resources offered to the Church by native people.[13] Only in this way can the alienation caused by feelings of cultural and racial inferiority be overcome. Vine Deloria applies to Indians Michael Harrington's thesis that the poor are conspicuous by their invisibility—noting, too, that Harrington never once mentions Indians in his book *The Other America*![14] In accord with Deloria's protestation, Church workers, Indian and non-Indian alike, are labouring to give native peoples a voice and a profile in the Church by means of the dynamically growing Tekakwitha Conference in the United States and a similar missionary conference in Canada. In attempting to come to grips with the problems of cross-cultural listening, these groups are discovering what a profound and disturbing reality the term 'inculturation' denotes.

The Church in the United States is also taking advocacy measures on behalf of native people. The Tekakwitha Conference itself experienced a profound and salutary shock as it struggled to respond through prayer and political assistance to a group of Guatemala natives who brought evidence of assassination and torture of Indians by the ruling powers in that country. The Society of Jesus in the United States has now assigned a full-time person to the Washington scene, to work on behalf of Native Americans in the offices of the Church and the halls of secular government. Perhaps, too, a recent document published by a joint United States-Canadian fact-finding task force in Chile has not been wasted on the American consciousness. This group reports on the gradual dwindling, often accompanied by violence, of the lands of the Mapuche tribe. A land law, based on the principle of individual ownership rather than communal needs, fragments the tribe to the extent that today the land owned by the Mapuche people is about one one-hundredth of the area held by the tribe before the arrival of the Conquistadores, and it continues to diminish.[15] Americans with any knowledge of their own frontier history will recognise here the fundamental principles of the Dawes Severalty Act of 1887. Whether the basic evil be simple greed, cultural insensitivity or virulent racism—whether in North or South America—the social calling of the Church seems quite clear: to help indigenous peoples to acquire power and profile, and to gain a base of self confidence from which they may be called to a deeper living of the gospel. Because of the deep religious nature of Indian life, one soon discovers that this 'social' apostolate is itself a religious and spiritual apostolate as well. Thus, in aiding the many struggles of these people, the Church itself may learn how to grow.

Notes

1. Cornelius J. Jaenen *Friend and Foe: Aspects of French-Amerindian Cultural Contact in the Sixteenth and Seventeenth Centuries* (New York 1976) p. 9.

2. *Ibid.* p. 34.

3. See my brief article on racism in *Commitment* (Washington: National Catholic Conference for Interracial Justice, 1979) 3-4.

4. Vine Deloria, Jr. *Custer Died for Your Sins* (New York 1969) p. 174.

5. *Ibid.* p. 175ff.

6. Karl Rahner, SJ 'Towards a Fundamental Interpretation of Vatican II' trans. Leo J. O'Donovan, SJ *Theological Studies,* 40, No. 4 (December 1979) 717.

7. *Statement of United States Catholic Bishops on American Indians* (Washington: United States Catholic Conference, 1977).

8. *Brothers and Sisters to Us: United States Bishops' Pastoral Letter on Racism in Our Day* (Washington: United States Catholic Conference, 14 November 1979) p. 14.

9. 'Racism—And How to Fight It' *Catholic Update* (Cincinnati, March 1980) 3.

10. *Pastoral On American Indians* §6.

11. Silvio Fittipaldi 'The Catholic Church and the American Indian' *Horizons* 5 (Spring 1978) 73-75. See also my 'A Reflection on "The Catholic Church and the American Indian"' *Horizons* 6 (Fall 1978) 255-258.

12. Juan Luis Segundo, SJ *The Hidden Motives of Pastoral Action* trans. John Drury aryknoll, New York 1978). This is Segundo's theme throughout the book.

13. On mutuality, see the fine article of David J. Bosch 'Towards True Mutuality: Exchanging the Same Commodities or Supplementing Each Other's Needs?' *Missiology* 6 No. 3 (July 1979) 283-296.

14. Deloria *op. cit.* p. 12.

15. *Mapuches: People of the Land* (Toronto: Inter-Church Committee on Human Rights in Latin America, Newsletter, Spring 1980) passim.

Francis McHugh

Churches and Racism:
A Report from England

'I REMAIN optimistic that we shall rise successfully to the challenge during the last two decades of the century and turn our ideal of justice into a reality. One reason for my optimism is the increasingly Christian involvement.'
David Lane, Chairman of the *Commission for Racial Equality*.[1]

1. INTRODUCTION

The issue of race and the problems connected with a multi-racialist society did not land suddenly in the lap of an inexperienced Britain[2] after the Second World War. There had been, in fact, a centuries-old experience of heavy immigration into this country. In the seventeenth and eighteenth centuries, 80,000 Huguenots came to this country from France in order to avoid political and religious persecution; then there was the well-known mass movement of the Irish into Britain after the potato famines of the 1840s; again, between 1875 and 1914 120,000 Jewish immigrants settled in England mostly in the East End of London; most surprisingly of all, it is estimated that in 1764 there were 20,000 Black people in London out of a population of 676,000.

Experience of immigration, however, did little to prepare either the nation or the churches to cope with the ignorance, prejudices, fears, tensions and even violence thrown up in the wake of the flood of immigrants, especially Black immigrants, coming into England in the 1950s and 1960s. The English response to the massive post-war Black immigration was embedded in a sense of racialist superiority which it has proved difficult to dispel. An inspection of British imperial and colonial history suggests that this deep-seated attitude stems from a political paternalism associated with the flag, and economic dominance connected with overseas trade and a religious superiority accompanying the missionary thrust of Christianity, particularly of the Church of England in India and Africa. The fundamental importance of this aspect of the race issue in England has been acknowledged recently in 'A statement by the British Council of Churches' Working Party on Britain as a Multi-racial Society': 'The basic issue is not a problem caused by Black people: the basic issue concerns the nature of British society as

70

a whole, and features of that society which have been there long before the recent phase of Black immigration.'[3]

2. THE NEW BLACK PRESENCE IN BRITAIN

Whichever way it is looked at—from the angle that large numbers of Black immigrants brought new problems or that they revealed problems which already existed—it soon became evident to politicians, policy-makers and to the public that the new immigrants were not going to be easily integrated into the host society, though their arrival in Britain was encouraged in order to help solve the problem of labour-shortage after the war. One million people left their homes in Africa and Asia and settled in England mostly in the city slums. There are now two million Black people in Britain—4 per cent of the population—and these are usually referred to as 'the immigrants' in spite of the fact that half of them are British-born and that they constitute only one-third of the immigrants who have come to Britain in the past thirty years. In their general presentation of the race issue in England, the Christian churches emphasise an important dimension of discrimination when they insist that the problem displays itself in an attitude to Black people and not to immigrants in general. As the Anglican Bishop of Liverpool says, 'I've been told that discrimination against Black people is no different from the way southerners might be treated in Yorkshire or Lancashire. That is wholly untrue.'[4]

Discrimination against the Black community is different. Out of the sizeable Black presence in England there is no Black trade union leader nor any Black chief executive; out of 130,000 policemen only 218 are Asian or West Indian; of white men with educational qualifications to degree standard 79 per cent are in professional or managerial positions, whereas only 31 per cent of those in ethnic minorities, possessing equivalent qualifications achieve comparable occupational status; and in 1973 the *Political and Economic Planning* research institute found that Black unskilled workers had a one in two chance of being discriminated against when applying for jobs. Add to all this the discrimination practised by local authorities in housing; the number of Black children in Educationally Sub-normal Schools; the belief in the Black communities that the police fail to protect them and that Stop and Search powers are used unfairly against them, and one begins to appreciate the size of the problem. Nor have the churches themselves been wholly blameless in the matter of discrimination. In a survey on Black children in Catholic schools, the Catholic Commission for Racial Justice found, 'that most Black Catholic families would like a Catholic education for their children but either because they apply too late to an overcrowded school, or because they fail to get the right information, or because they are not in the mainstream of parish life, all but the most persistent fail to get places'. But the form of discrimination which most readily rouses fear and violence is the new fascism which has begun to flourish in Britain. Its most public expression is to be found in the activities of the National Front, with its stated aims of repatriating coloured immigrants or the creation of apartheid in this country, the prohibition of mixed marriages, tightening up on law and order, severe restriction of State welfare benefits, an all-white Commonwealth and withdrawal from the European Economic Community.

3. THE RESPONSE OF GOVERNMENT

The debate about race relations in Britain has been overshadowed by the issue of immigration control. Under the British Nationality Act 1948 all 'British subjects/

F

Commonwealth citizens' had the right to move in and out of the United Kingdom. For the first decade or so after their arrival little attention was paid to the Black immigrants but the Notting Hill riots of 1958 alerted the government and the public to the danger that was developing, almost unnoticed, in their midst. The response of government was to pass Immigration Acts 1962, 1968 and 1971, which have had the effect of cutting away the categories of Commonwealth citizens and limiting their conditions of entry. The philosophy behind legislation is that immigration is the chief obstacle to better race relations—a view still represented in the Report of the Commons Select Committee on Race Relations and Immigration 1978. In this sense legislation has been a negative factor in race relations policy, at least up until the 1976 Race Relations Act, which passed stronger laws to eliminate racial discrimination and promote equality of opportunity. Perhaps the most useful achievement of this recent Act has been the setting-up of the Commission for Racial Equality. This does not mean that the earlier negative approach of the government has given way to the more positive direction of the 1976 Act. In 1977, the Labour Government's Green Paper 'British Nationality Law: a discussion of possible changes' proposed a redefinition of British nationality and citizenship. In 1981, the Conservative Government introduced a British Nationality Bill which, if passed, will have the effect of putting British citizenship on a racial basis: the categories of 'British Overseas Citizens' and 'Citizens of the British Dependent Territories' will have British passports but no rights of entry. It seems that discrimination may be finally built into the very fabric of the law.

4. THE RESPONSE OF THE CHURCHES

The churches at first paid little attention to the new Black work-force which had taken up unskilled manual jobs and low-paid service employment. And ignorance of the new Black-presence was matched by neglect of it. Confession of this early failure has been a consistent feature of Church discussion of race relations: 'Most of all their disillusionment has been occasioned not simply by the failure of the Christian Church to rise to their defence and officially champion their cause to secure justice and equality of treatment, but by the failure of ordinary people in the churches to make them feel welcome and wanted when they attempt to worship God alongside their new white neighbours.'[5] The extent of this neglect may be measured by the remarkable growth of the new Black-led churches in Britain.

The survey, Colour and Citizenship,[6] documented the widespread ignorance in Britain about Black immigrants. It also showed that when race riots broke out in Notting Hill in 1958 there were no experts available to give enlightenment or advice. It was four years more before the government made any response, and then only in the wholly inappropriate 1962 Act. In the case of the Christian churches it took them two decades to recognise new forms of responsibility in a multi-racial society. Only at the beginning of the 1970s did they begin to organise themselves at an official level to meet the new challenges. In February 1971, for instance, the British Council of Churches set up its Community and Race Relations Unit; and in the same year the Roman Catholic Church established its Catholic Commission for Racial Justice. The foundation of many unofficial groups, such as All Faiths for One Race, Christians against Racism and Fascism and the Evangelical Race Relations Group came after official initiatives. Two dimensions of race relations work in the British churches have been prominent: the ecumenical nature of Christian effort and the close co-operation with secular agencies. Most of the mainstream churches—even though they have their own specialised race relations committee—work through the Community and Race Relations Unit of the British Council of Churches. Only the Church of England has no special committee, and until recently its Board of Social Responsibility worked mostly through the CRRU on which it was heavily represented. In 1980, however, the Board of Social Responsibility did begin to employ a full-time worker, the Reverend Kenneth Leech, to work with the Projects Fund of the BCC. The Catholic Commission for Racial Justice and the Friends Community Relations Committee are not integrated formally into the CRRU, but they do co-operate closely and sit jointly on many inter-church and secular agencies. The extent and effectiveness of this co-operation with secular agencies is rare in the history of contact between British churches and public policy bodies. Perhaps only in respect of housing problems has there been any comparable co-operation. On race issues the churches work closely with the government-established *Commission for Racial Equality* and *Action Group on Immigration and Nationality*, the *Joint Council for the Welfare of Immigrants* and even with the more extremist *Race Today*.

5. ACTIVITIES OF THE BRITISH COUNCIL OF CHURCHES

The main concern of the Community and Race Relations Unit has been with education, first of all of church leaders themselves, and then with the wider Church and society. The work began in 1973 with the setting-up of a Working Party to investigate objectives for a new multi-racial society in Britain, to identify the forces at work here and to articulate principles for action. This was followed in 1979 by the signing of an Affirmation and Commitment on the Christian's response to racism. 300,000 signatures were obtained and taken to the Home Office as evidence of support for government policies outlawing racism. The most recent initiative in educating the churches was the meeting in summer 1980 of thirty church leaders to seek a common mind on how the churches can respond more effectively to the challenge on racism. All the mainstream churches participated in this initiative and directed their attention to effort at the level of the *local* congregation and at the *national* and *international* levels.

6. THE PROJECTS FUND

One effective strategy which the BCC has adopted for educating the membership of local churches and for achieving some direct influence at local level has been the Projects Fund. This allocates £100,000 each year to 100 different projects (at home, not overseas) varying from youth clubs to law centres, and from skills-training workshops to Matthews Meeting Place, which is a parish church in Brixton, imaginatively converted and now serving as a community centre. The Director of CCRU views the Projects Fund as a vital part of the BCC's work for the future of British multi-racial society. The recent appointment of the Reverend Kenneth Leech by the Board of Social Responsibility of the Church of England is to serve the dual purpose of raising £100,000 from local Anglican churches to finance the Fund, and, at the same time, to raise the level of consciousness of the local congregations about Christian duties in respect of race relations.

7. PUBLIC POLICY INITIATIVES

It is difficult to estimate the influence of churches on government policy and on public attitudes, but the CRRU has worked to achieve as much unity as possible in speaking with a clear and unequivocal voice on issues of race. The Director acknowledges organisational weaknesses for public policy operations, and a lack of success in taking on the media, but he does claim that the strong stand taken recently against the government's Nationality Bill has forced the government to give further thought to proposed legislation.

8. JOINT WORKING PARTY OF WHITE-LED AND BLACK-LED CHURCHES

Since the Second World War, 750 congregations belonging to 150 Black-led churches have sprung up in Britain. Though their very existence is something of a reproach to the white-led churches, attempts are now being made at co-operation. The Working Party, established in late 1976, has presented three constructive reports, *Coming Together in Christ*, *Building Together in Christ* and *Learning in Partnership*.[7] In addition to the general educational value of this work, there have been tangible results in sharing churches, and, most notably, in theological education. The *Project in Partnership between Black and White*, housed at Selly Oak Colleges and backed by the University of Birmingham, is successfully completing its first two-year Certificate in Theology course this year.

9. OTHER CHURCHES AND OTHER INITIATIVES

The Catholic Commission for Racial Justice and the Friends Community Relations Committee, while co-operating with the BCC, conduct independent work in the whole field of race relations. The Quakers, for example, have made detailed investigations of fascism and racism in Britain and have published a detailed study offering guidance to Christians in this matter. The CCRJ has been a strong and effective force in the field, first, because structurally it is not at all bureaucratised and is highly flexible, and, second, because it is able to call on the guidance of a small number of people who have become highly expert since the beginning of the 1970s. In addition to its educational work, carried out through its high quality publications, it has tackled hard issues: immigration policy, revision of nationality law, the police, public order and the penal system. Its work is thorough and analytic. In 1979 and 1981 it advised the Roman Catholic hierarchy, which then issued a strong statement on the Nationality Bill, whose progress through parliament has been slowed down for more careful consideration.

An important development since 1978 has been the appointment of a full-time Regional Fieldworker and a part-time London Fieldworker with the role of helping the Church in local areas to adapt its ministry to the needs of a multi-racial and multi-cultural society. In the case of the Roman Catholic Church in Britain, there is a particular need for fieldwork of this kind, since the social cohesion, almost ghetto mentality, of Irish Catholicism in England has resulted in a social, and not simply religious, exclusiveness, which may explain the resistance to the anti-racialist stand of the Catholic Bishops at the recent National Pastoral Congress.[8]

A recent and unique initiative has been the formation, during 1980, of a working party to begin examining theological concepts which may be relevant to Church involvement in multi-racial society. The initial theme for study is 'White Church in a Multi-racial Society'. 'This decision means that the starting point and focus for our reflection will be the historical fact that the mainline Christian churches in this country are predominantly white. In the Catholic Church this expresses itself through a certain Anglo-Irish cultural dominance in some parishes, the phenomenon of Blacks feeling unwelcome, the development of Black-led churches, and the phenomenon of mono-racial church schools in many places.'[9]

CONCLUSION

If the work of the churches is to be effective in a multi-racial society, there must be a match of Church effort to the social realities of the nation. In that the British churches direct their education to dispelling any sense of white superiority and emphasise the equality of all men, thus identifying and aiming to correct a fundamental misconception about race in British society; in that they attack discrimination in all its forms, criticising themselves as well as the wider society by corrective education and by using the Projects Fund as an instrument of positive discrimination in favour of Black initiatives; in their opposition to Immigration Acts and the Nationality Bill; and, finally, in their work at local, national and international level, including the BCC's courageous co-operation with the World Council of Churches' *Programme to Combat Racism*—in all these ways the British churches justify the optimism in their efforts recorded in the opening quotation to this report.

Notes

1. British Council of Churches *Reflections on Race: analysis* by three prominent churchmen, p. 1 (London 1979).

2. The Report, though from England, touches on the wider British scene. The contents, however, relate mostly to England, where the bulk of the Black population resides.

3. BCC *The New Black Presence in Britain: a Christian scrutiny*, p. 7 (London 1976).

4. *Ibid.* p. 4.

5. C. S. Hill and A. Mathews *Race: a Christian symposium* (London 1968) p. 174.

6. E. J. B. Rose *Colour and Citizenship* (Oxford 1969).

7. BCC 1978-1980.

8. See *The Tablet*, 19 and 26 July 1980 for criticism by Catholics. In the editorial for 2 August it is suggested that 'if this means that if the level of prejudice among Catholics is comparable to that of the wider community, then in this respect the leadership of the Church in this country has failed' pp. 743-744.

9. CCRJ *Annual Report* 1980 p. 3.

G

Jean Pihan

The Church and Racism in France

1. RACISM IN FRANCE

IN METROPOLITAN France at least six million people risk being the object of racist attitudes. There are four groups made up almost entirely of French citizens, the Jews (700,000, including 400,000 of North African origin), the gipsies and other 'travelling people' (150,000-200,000), the 'coloured people' from the overseas departments and territories (400,000) and the 'Moslem French', who chose to come to France at the time of Algerian independence (300,000).

Then there are the foreigners (over 4 million), mostly manual workers, who come either from European countries (Central and Eastern Europe, Italy, Spain, Portugal) or from North Africa (including 800,000 Algerians) and Black Africa, and now also the refugees from South East Asia. Of the total about 1 million are under fifteen years of age.

In addition to the risk of having to face more or less racist attitudes on the part of certain French people, foreign workers and their families are subject to legislative or administrative measures introduced for economic reasons or, allegedly, for the sake of 'law and order', which are sometimes applied by the police authorities in an indisputably racist and inhuman way. The same is true of the 'travelling people'. In recent years the situation of the children of immigrant parents has also seemed increasingly precarious. There has been some improvement as a result of the political changes in France in spring 1981. Arbitrary expulsions were stopped and the situation of the children of immigrants has been eased. Nevertheless, despite the government's good intentions about abolishing all 'State racism', much still remains to be done.

Are the French people racist?

For a considerable part of the population, especially in rural areas, the question hardly arises, for lack of contact, except with gipsies, towards whom the normal attitude is suspicion.

At all levels of society attitudes can be observed which derive less from racism than from chauvinism or xenophobia, a feeling of French superiority, suspicion of foreigners, 'fear of the other' as unknown and because it is felt that 'they have a different way of life'. There is also the attitude of economic defence: foreigners are accused of causing unemployment. These attitudes easily become racism when their objects are 'Arabs' or coloured people (even French citizens). They may extend to serious and even criminal actions. Since the majority of potential victims of racism are immigrant workers, the main thrust of the problems raised by their presence is not racist but economic and political. Racism comes in only as a dimension which aggravates French complaints about them; it weighs heavier the further the nationalities or 'races' (the term is very ambiguous) are from the French 'type'.

Finally, a small, noisy minority, usually described as 'extreme right-wing', fosters aggressive racism and virulent anti-Semitism. It is supported by various publications and by theorists of an allegedly scientific racism which is not without links with the crude racism of the nineteenth century, the school of the Action Française and even Nazi racism. Its manifestations range from graffiti to bombings. 'Integrist' Catholics have a curious tolerance for it, though some of its 'leaders' have no hesitation in attacking 'Judeo-Christianity', which, they claim, has perverted the western world and bastardised the 'Indo-European race'. They espouse a neo-paganism.

2. THE FRENCH CHURCH AND RACISM

The Church means on the one hand the hierarchy and on the other the Christian people, among whom we should distinguish between the 'practising' minority and the mass of the baptised with no more than fairly loose ties with the Church. Between the two are found the 'movements' and the various institutions (education, charities, etc.) and the explicitly Christian press.

(a) The hierarchy

Its attitude, at least since the liberation, has been irreproachable, both in racism in general and on anti-Semitism in particular.

The bishops have been criticised for failure to come out in large numbers in open defence of the Jews during the Nazi occupation, but since 1945 there have been numerous, often vigorous, statements. To mention only a few, there have been the pastoral letter of Cardinal Liénart (Lille) against anti-Semitism in 1960, the 1968 statements by Cardinal Marty (Paris): 'France is in danger of racism', and by Cardinal Etchegaray (Marseilles) in 1978. The bishops have made frequent statements in support of immigrants and in the Episcopal Conference's recent note on the occasion of the 1981 presidential elections the defence of the rights of immigrant workers was listed as one of the most important points to which Catholics should pay attention.

The connection between the problems of immigration and the racist attitudes of the average French person and of the public authorities is such that the Episcopal Commission on Migrations cannot avoid making frequent statements against racism when dealing with the situation to which immigrant workers are subjected. On its initiative, since 1970, many immigrant aid organisations have been set up or co-ordinated; the chaplains of the different nationalities and of the overseas departments and territories have come to the defence of their nationals at the same time as looking after their religious lives. A national organisation of chaplains for gipsies and travellers has been set up and a bishop appointed so that these groups do not feel 'strangers in the Church' as they are—alas—all too often in the city.

The highest authorities of the Reformed Churches and the French Protestant Federation are taking similar action to the Catholic hierarchy, and often in concert with it.

(*b*) **The Christian People**

They are frequently 'alerted' to the danger of racism or anti-Semitism, by the bishops, supported by the parish clergy, and the Christian press.

Because the bishops also make very frequent statements on other violations of human rights and the clergy readily backs up these statements, a certain number of 'traditional' practising Catholics feel that 'There's really too much done for *those people*', and claim that 'it's politics and not religion'. The mass of the French people—practising or not—who take little notice of Christianity, are still far from having realised the social implications of faith. Their normal attitudes differ little, as regards xenophobia, racism or anti-Semitism—and indeed Third World issues—from those of the rest of the population. If one discounts the activists in the various organisations and all those influenced by reading the Christian press, the teachings of the popes and the bishops have little hold on the majority of people, whose immediate reactions spring from their prejudices and their political opinions. At the very most they have a vague impression of 'highly excusable culpability' when they are reminded of all this; this appears in the well-known formula, 'I'm not racist, but. . . .'

It should be said that there are signs of some progress in these areas among younger people. It is not clear that this progress is the result of Church influence. Daily contacts with young foreigners, especially in educational contexts, go a long way to accounting for it. And young Christians are much more active and generous, take part in many more fruitful initiatives, than their elders.

(*c*) **The press, the organisations and the institutions**

The general interest Catholic press consists of one daily paper, and several weeklies and monthlies. There is also a large number of provincial Catholic papers and standard parish bulletin sheets with a large circulation. The Protestant press includes one daily and a variety of other publications. Like that of the hierarchy, the attitude of this press in the fight against racism and anti-Semitism is excellent. It denounces evils, including what there is to criticise in government policy, it faithfully reports the Church's constant position and it publicises positive achievements. Hardly a week passes without reason for satisfaction with its statements. It is noteworthy, however, that the further to the 'right' a publication is, the more strangely silent it is about issues of racism, as about most of the social injustices in France or (certain) other parts of the world.

The Catholic Action organisations have an openly anti-racist attitude. Nevertheless, the positions of some of them, those closest to the working class, are not always comfortable with regard to the positions to be taken on immigration. It is possible to be anti-racist and fraternal towards individuals and at the same time circumspect with regard to the effect of the presence of these millions of foreigners on the economic life of the country in a time of industrial recession and unemployment. But the point need not be pressed.

The Catholic scout movement, and in particular its female wing, is prominent in initiatives for fraternisation with young people from foreign countries. The same is true of the 'Enfance missionnaire' and children's Catholic Action, which are closely linked to MIDADE (the international movement for the children's apostolate). In Catholic education a great effort has been made for over thirty years to clean up openly or covertly anti-Semitic textbooks. The same has been done with catechisms.

There is—happily—no denominational anti-racist movement in France. Christians are active in fair numbers in both of the two big non-denominational anti-racist organisations, MRAP (Mouvement contre le racisme et pour l'amitié entre les peuples) and LICRA (Ligue internationale contre le racisme et l'antisémitisme). Much is also done to break down racist prejudices by the institutions which fight under-development and the egoism of the 'have' nations (Comité catholique contre la faim et pour le développement, Cimade), work for peace (Pax Christi) or mobilise Catholics for charitable work (Secours Catholique). The same is true of the various missionary organisations and their publications. Missionaries and missions today present a totally different appearance from half a century ago. A characteristic common to all these efforts is to recognise 'the other' as a partner and not as an object of help.

Finally, mention should be made of the discreet work of the organisations specialising in relations with Judaism, Amitié judéo-chrétienne, Service international de documentation judéo-chrétienne. Friendly dialogue has replaced anathemas. Something similar is beginning to take shape in relations with Islam. It has often been the action of the clergy and Christians that Moslems (the second largest religious group in France) have been able to obtain places of worship. For the gipsies there is the Association of Our Lady of the Gipsies, and the other, non-denominational organisations are in practice run by Christians.

A summary might look something like this:

The situation in France is marked by a still disturbing degree of racism, connected primarily with the problem of foreign workers, which the authorities seem incapable of resolving other than by drastic measures not free of racism. Anti-Semitism is less than in the past, but still present below the surface. The French Church is very clearly anti-racist in its hierarchy, in its institutions and in the bulk of its means of expression.

The Christian people in France (though how far is that description accurate?) are fairly indifferent to these issues and still imbued with prejudices, except for a very active minority. It is a huge mass difficult to shift.

Addresses

Episcopal commission on migration, pastoral organisations for minorities: Secrétariat de la Commission épiscopale des migrations: 269bis rue du Faubourg Saint-Antoine, 75011 Paris.

Gipsies: Aumônerie nationale des Gitans, 5 rue d'Estienne d'Orves, 93500 Pantin.

Christians and Jews: Amitié judéo-chrétienne, 11 rue d'Enghien, 75010 Paris.

Anti-racism: Mouvement contre le racisme et pour l'amitié entre les peuples, 89 rue Oberkampf, 75011 Paris; Ligue internationale contre le racisme et l'antisémitisme, 40 rue de Paradis, 75011 Paris.

Translated by Francis McDonagh

Helmut Erlinghagen

Report from Japan

THE FACT that the report from Japan comes at the end of the symposium may be due to the fact that Catholics in Japan make up less than 0·4 per cent of the population. On the other hand Japan is an economic power of the first rank and the undisputed leader of the non-communist group of Far Eastern nations consisting of South Korea, Taiwan, Hong Kong and Singapore. As regards racism, too, Japan occupies a special position. Not only has it long ago left behind the tutelage of whites, it has even developed its own exclusiveness, and if the term 'racism' has any application to Japan it is to this that it might apply.

The first period of contact between whites and Japan lasted from 1545 to about 1640. The European maritime nations of the time who came to Japan did not seriously contemplate an attempt at conquest because the warlike character and the numbers of the population—with Kyoto said to already have half a million inhabitants—seemed to rule this out. Despite the general admiration for things Japanese shown by the missionaries who entered the country after the arrival of Francis Xavier in 1549, native clergy were for a long time not found in the higher orders. The plenipotentiary P. Valignano, who held office in Japan for the first time in 1579, secured the entry of Japanese into the higher orders. Nonetheless there were no Japanese bishops, who might have inspired the oppressed Christians during the later persecution. The result was that at the end of this catacomb existence of 250 years the priests died out.

It may have been an attempt to defend itself at least verbally against a suspected superiority of the whites which led the Japanese society of the time to label them 'the barbarians from the South', *nambanjin*—from the South, because the whites did approach Japan from the South, by the Malacca route. Even today the customs and clothing of the whites of the so-called 'Christian century' are clearly visible on the 'painted wall screens dealing with the southern barbarians', the *nambanyôbu*.

Partly as a result of civilising influences from China, which at this time was almost the equal of the West in many ways, in this first period of contact with whites Japan at no time risked losing its independence. The situation during the second encounter with the whites was very different.

Relying on the clear technological superiority of his fleet, the American admiral Perry in 1853 demanded the opening of the harbours. This was followed by the signature of treaties with the United States, England, Russia, Holland and other countries which the Japanese called 'the unequal treaties'. The most important aspect of discrimination was that foreigners in certain harbours were left under the jurisdiction of their own officials and, if they broke Japan's laws, they were dealt with by their own courts.

Japanese resistance to these privileges of the whites was embodied in the ideology of *jôi-sonnô* ('Drive out the barbarians, honour the emperor.'). This had two main demands, first, that more power should be given to the emperor and not to the shogun, who still held real power, and, second, the expulsion of foreigners. The second aim was soon recognised not only as difficult, but also as inadvisable, since foreigners provided many teachers. Contact with the whites and the use of their knowledge to defend the country seemed to be the need of the moment. A new slogan, *wakon-yôsai* (Japanese soul and western knowledge) finally proved to be the expression of the real intellectual basis of modern Japan.

In 1899 the 'unequal treaties' were revised, a step which laid the foundations for Japan's rise to become a modern military power. Japan's ability to match the imperialism of the time had been displayed even earlier in the war with China (1894-95), and it was given another notable demonstration in the Russo-Japanese war of 1904-05. Japan now had a say in anything that happened in the Far East. It gradually absorbed Korea, a great nation to which Japan owed an immense debt as a channel of culture. Japan's humiliating treatment of the Koreans and the amazing attempt completely to absorb this whole nation, politically, economically and above all linguistically, an attempt frustrated only by the outcome of the Second World War, is a unique example of radical late colonialism.

Arrogance was also the main feature of Japan's attitude to China, the undoubted creative source of culture in the Far East. The twenty-one demands with which Japan finally confronted China on 21 January 1915 during the First World War would have made the Middle Kingdom a Japanese vassal. When diplomatic relations with the Kuomintang government were broken off in 1930, the Japanese attitude was summed up in a phrase which also said much about Japan: 'A government of the Chinese people cannot be recognised as a partner in negotiations.'

The situation inside the Catholic Church in modern Japan cannot be considered in connection with the political attitudes of this great nation because the Church was and is numerically so tiny as to make any comparison meaningless. Nevertheless it should be mentioned that during the first phase of missionary activity, which may be regarded as ending with the Second World War, bishops were drawn predominantly from the missionary orders, from the Franciscans, the Jesuits, the Dominicans and, above all, from the members of the Missions étrangères de Paris. Only in Nagasaki, from 1927, was there a Japanese bishop, followed in 1938 by a Japanese archbishop for Tokio. Today all seventeen bishops are Japanese. The provision of numerous bishops in the Japanese Church is one indication that discrimination on the part of whites is non-existent. It is somewhat surprising that none of the missionaries who adopted Japanese nationality many years ago was previously raised to the episcopate, even though the majority of priests in Japan were for a long time foreigners. This is all the more amazing in view of the generous attitude of the universities in appointments. The only condition is that a person suitable for a senior appointment should, as part of this suitability, be a person who will not disturb the harmony of social relations (*wa*) which is so highly valued in Japan. As a result non-Japanese are found at all levels of the staff of universities, colleges and even high schools, and alternate with Japanese as necessary.

The old 'predominance' of whites in the Church survives only in insignificant details, occasionally preserved out of piety or perhaps a shaky sense of humour. For a long time the sisters of three leading Tokio girls' schools were addressed, according to the origin of the congregation, as *Mother*, *Mamère* or *Madre*, even in the case of Japanese nuns. The Japanese are unaffected by the habit of German missionaries using Japanese nouns in their 'mission German' with the article which the equivalent German word would have: 'die *daigaku* (university)', 'der *Fuji*' and 'das *kempo* (basic law)'. The French group regularly receive high French decorations for services to French culture. Southern Europe has left the 'Catholic custom' of the siesta, which is otherwise unknown in Japan.

In the western industrial nations people still remember the groups of travelling Japanese who constantly visited these countries to study every detail. After asking innumerable questions and taking innumerable notes, they would sit together in their hotel to exchange and consolidate their impressions. Today Japanese newspapers report the increasingly frequent visits of groups of foreigners who travel round Japan and do exactly the same in reverse. Japan is the industrial and economic wonderland whose great achievements are due principally to its superb organisation.

The unusual group specific behaviour is a product of history. It tolerates no obstinate exceptions: 'the nail that sticks out must be knocked in.' The exclusiveness of Japanese organisation can be described as racism in the broadest sense of the word. Because the language is also really difficult, and much is expressed in nuances, the Japanese group seems almost impossible to infiltrate. In fact, Japanese among themselves are very often open and discussion (from which women are excluded) is very vigorous. The underlying idea is perhaps that the extended family has lost its function since the end of the war and that the firm has taken over its functions. Power and responsibility are distributed in a diffuse way, as the environmental trials have clearly demonstrated. Decision-making is prepared by circulars (*ringisho*), which are passed from the lowest level to the middle and from there to the highest and then to the 'chief', who then has no choice but to ratify the general will. The firm behaves like a family which develops talents with patience and tolerates mistakes with the same patience.

But initiative, freedom of thought and delight in innovation are not the only values fostered and protected by the firm; there is also job security, which to some extent provides the secure framework within which dynamic energies can develop. Just as in a family no-one is 'disinherited', except under quite unusually and shocking circumstances, no Japanese company dismisses anyone unless a really serious crime has been committed. Any dismissal, or even the threat of one, brings the company union on to the scene, rightly believing that a precedent is being created here, that fundamentally the management is threatening all jobs. It is the only issue on which unions react so sharply.

Because of the difficulty of getting to grips with the unique features of Japanese organisation, and because it is so delicate, it is easy to see why the Japanese are particularly eager to press on with the development of robots. Robots do not disturb anything; they can be precisely predicted, indeed programmed, which is not the case with foreign workers and still less with managers determined to follow quite different principles. These have to be excluded; they are disruptive. That is racism in the broadest sense of the word or, better, an exclusiveness specific to Japan.

This behaviour was described above as the product of history (one reason why it is so difficult to imitate). In the cultural history of modern Japan the emphasis on inter-personal relations, indeed its equation with the good as such, is expressed most clearly in the philosophy of Watsuji Tetsurô (1889-1960). Morality is essentially *aidagara* (being among), the relationship of person to person, and only the self-denial that this involves makes possible the insertion of the individual into society. Watsuji regarded the nation as the end result of this process, and was thus in harmony with the Japanese world of his time, and he will soon I venture to predict, be felt to be modern once more. Nishida Kitarô (1870-1945), a cleverer thinker, while aware of the irrational elusiveness, sensitivity and exclusiveness of the Japanese character, presses beyond all this to reach an ultimate Japanese honesty, which enables them 'to get to the root of things'. This is a feature which must include the ability to overcome what I have called racism in the broadest sense. Truth is greater than the individual, but it is also greater than the nation.

Many Japanese feel unable to reconcile joining our Church with this honesty. Problems of belief are becoming greater throughout the world, and therefore particularly so in well-informed Japanese society. Issues of morality, particularly marital and family morality, seem an insuperable obstacle. The provisions of canon law, though the educated Japanese know them only from hearsay, give our Church the reputation of being *keishikitei*, pedantic and legalistic. There is still no sign in the Church of the atmosphere of widespread, free and thoroughly honest discussion.

There is still no structure of job security without threat until death, and the diffuse decision-making process is still unthinkable. Already, however, the managers of large European and American firms are flocking to Japan to learn. Japan as teacher: who would have thought it a hundred years ago when the colonial danger was acute? Should we, too, not begin to follow the children of this world, whose wisdom was, after all, prophesied, and be taught, at least lessons for our activities in Japan itself, though also perhaps, who knows, a new formula of world-wide application?

Translated by Francis McDonagh

Contributors

JOHANNES BROSSEDER is professor of systematic theology at Bonn and in charge of teaching ecumenical theology at Munich. His publications include *Ökumenische Theologie. Geschichte—Probleme* (1967), and *Luthers Stellung zu den Juden im Spiegel seiner Interpreten* (1973). He has edited the *Internationale Ökumenische Bibliographie* from volume 10/11 onwards. He has contributed numerous articles on questions of ecumenical and fundamental theology to journals and symposia.

ALAN DAVIES was born in Montreal, Quebec. He is a graduate of McGill University and of Union Theological Seminary, New York, and was post-doctoral fellow at Hebrew Union College, Cincinnati. He is an ordained minister of the United Church of Canada, and is associate professor of religious studies at Victoria College in the University of Toronto. He has written *Anti-semitism and the Christian Mind* (New York 1969) and edited *Anti-semitism and the Foundations of Christianity* (New York 1979).

MARIASUSAI DHAVAMONY, SJ, was ordained in Kurseong, India, in 1958, and is professor of Hinduism and of the history of religions at the Gregorian University, Rome. He is a licentiate in theology, doctor of philosophy of the Gregorian University and doctor of philosophy (Oriental religions) of Oxford University. He is editor of *Studia Missionalia* and *Documenta Missionalia* and has written many books and articles.

ENRIQUE DUSSEL was born in Argentina in 1934. With a degree in theology and a doctorate in philosophy, he lectures on ethics and Church history in Mexico. He is president of the study commission on Church history of Latin America, and a founder member of the Ecumenical Association of Third World Theologians. He is the author of numerous works on theology and the history of the Church in Latin America, among which the following have recently appeared in English: *Ethics and the Theology of Liberation* (1978); *History of the Church in Latin America, 1492-1980* (1981); *Papers for Liberation Theology* (1981).

VIRGIL ELIZONDO was born in San Antonio, Texas. He did higher studies at the Ateneo University (Manila), at the East Asian Pastoral Institute (Manila) and at the Institut Catholique (Paris). After three years of parochial work, he became director of the Confraternity of Christian Doctrine (1966-1970) and dean of studies at Assumption Seminary (1967-1972). Since 1971 he has been president of the Mexican American Cultural Center in San Antonio. His publications include *A Search for Meaning in Life and Death* (Manila 1971); *Hombre, ¿Quien Eres Tu?* (Mexico City 1971); *Christianity and Culture* (Huntington 1975); *Hombres en Marcha* (1975); *Mestizaje—The dialectic of cultural birth and the gospel* (San Antonio 1978); *The Human Quest* (Huntington 1977); *La Morenita, Evangelizer of the Americas* (San Antonio 1980). He has been co-editor of the issue of Practical Theology of *Concilium* since 1979 and author of numerous other articles in various books and periodicals.

HELMUT ERLINGHAGEN, SJ, was born in 1915 in Hagen, Germany, entered the Society of Jesus in 1935 in Holland and went to Japan in 1937. Apart from studying for three years in the USA to do his doctorate under Dietrich von Hildebrand, he lived in Japan until 1971, spending most of his time teaching at Sophia University, Tokyo. Apart from setting up a language school for Japanese, he taught ethics at the university and built up a network of study groups for the study of Christianity in Tokyo and other cities. He has personally received some 1,500 Japanese into the Church, most of them students whom he formed into an association with its own newspaper. For ten years this group ran a house of leisure which registered some 20,000 overnight stays a year. He now teaches Japanology and ethics at the Johannes Gutenberg University in Bingen, West Germany.

CAIN FELDER is currently assistant professor of New Testament Studies at the Howard University Divinity School in Washington, DC, USA. He received his BA in philosophy and classics at Howard University in 1966, the DipTheol from Oxford University (Mansfield College) in 1968, the MDiv degree from Union Theological Seminary (New York) in 1969 and the MPhil (religion) from Columbia University in 1978. His doctoral dissertation is entitled 'Law, Wisdom and Justice in the Epistle of James'. From 1978-1981, Mr Felder served as instructor in New Testament at Princeton Theological Seminary, Princeton, New Jersey. He is an ordained minister in the United Methodist Church (New York Annual Conference) and served as the national director of that denomination's Black caucus from 1969-1972. He has also taught at the following colleges and universities: Morgan State University (Baltimore), Coppin State College (Baltimore) and the City University of New York (Hunter College). Mr Felder has published book reviews and articles in such journals as *The Union Quarterly Review, Theology Today* and *Interim*.

ROGER-HENRI GUERRAND was born in 1923. He holds a doctor's degree in history and is a member of Paul-Henry Chombart de Lauwe's research group at the Ecole des Hautes Etudes en Sciences Sociales in Paris. He specialises in the history of the daily life of the urban working class. At one time he was the national director of the French Student Christian Movement and is one of the founder members of Culture et Liberté, which is one of the pioneer movements of popular education in France. He has written, among other things, *Mémoires du Métro*, *La Conquête des vacances*, *Les Origines du logement social en France* and *Brève histoire du Service Social*.

FRANCIS McHUGH was born in 1931 in England and is a Roman Catholic priest. He gained degrees in the Universities of both Oxford and Cambridge. He was Howard lecturer for 1981 in the University of Sussex on the topic 'The changing social role of the Roman Catholic Church in England, 1958-1980: a political push or theological push?' and is currently Maurice Reckitt Fellow of the University of Sussex. He has written *Aspects of the Social Role of the Roman Catholic Church in England* (Brussels 1979) and 'Comments on *The Church of Scotland: an economic survey*' in *The Economic Journal* (summer 1981).

CHUKWUDUM BARNABAS OKOLO is a diocesan priest from Nnobi, Nigeria, who is now senior lecturer in philosophy at the University of Nigeria, Nsukka, Nigeria. He took his master's degree in classics from Fordham University, New York, and a master's degree and a PhD in philosophy from the Catholic University, Washington, DC. He later did post-doctoral studies in liberation theology in St Michael's College, University of Toronto, Canada, where he also held a two-year teaching fellowship. His published works include *Racism: A Philosophic Probe* (New York 1974), *Marxian and Christian Ethics* (Kenya 1978), *African Church and Signs of the Times: A Socio-Political Analysis* (Kenya 1978) as well as many scholarly articles.

JEAN PIHAN is a priest in the congregation of the Sons of Charity. He was born in Cherbourg in 1912. Fr Pihan has been associated with a number of Catholic organisations concerned with education and child welfare. He was director of the Union des Oeuvres Catholiques de France and editor of the periodicals *Educateurs*, and *Educations paroissiales*. He has been national chaplain to Children's Catholic Action (Coeurs Vaillants—Ames Vaillantes), national director of the Union pontificale missionaire and vice-president of the Paris branch of the Oeuvres pontificales missionnaires. At present he is the archivist of his congregation and a religious journalist, with columns in *La Croix* and *Témoignage Chrétien*. He is also vice-president of the anti-racist organisation *Mouvement contre le racisme et pour l'amitié entre les peuples* (MRAP). Fr Pihan's writings on this subject include *La Largeur d'esprit* (1955), *L'Eglise et le racisme*, a special issue of the collection *Réponses Chrétiennes* (1968), both out of print.

DEOTIS ROBERTS was appointed president of the Interdenominational Theo-logical Center on 1 August 1980. He is a magna cum laude graduate of Johnson C. Smith University (AB). He also holds degrees from Shaw University (BD), Hartford Seminary Foundation (BD), Hartford Seminary (STM), and the University of Edinburgh, Scotland (PhD). Most recently he was a professor of theology at Howard University School of Religion and editor of the school's publication, *The Journal of Religious Thought*. He is also the former dean of religion at Virginia Union School of Theology and Georgia Baptist College, and he was the director of religious life and activities at Shaw University, where he served a term as college minister, and has served as co-director of the Annual Conference of Black Theologians. He has pursued professional study at Cambridge University, and has been Lilly Foundation Fellow in Christianity and Politics at Duke University, Fellow in South Asian Studies at the University of Wisconsin, Ford Foundation Faculty Fellow in South Asian Religion and Philosophy at University of Chicago, University of California, and the University of Wisconsin. Dr Roberts was Study-Travel Fellow in Asian Religions of the Society of Religion in Higher Education; a Fellow of the American Association of Theological Schools doing post-doctoral studies at Harvard Divinity School; on the Ford Foundation Faculty Development Seminar on East Asia at the University of Michigan, among others. His books include: *Faith and Reason in Pascal, Bergson and James* (1962); *From Puritanism to Platonism in Seventeenth-Century England* (1968); *Liberation and Reconciliation: A Black Theology* (1971); *Quest for a Black Theology* (1971); *Extending Redemption and Reconciliation* (1973); *A Black Political Theology* (1974); *Roots of a Black Future* (1980); *A Theological Commentary on the Sullivan Principles* (1980); and *Christian Beliefs* (1981).

RUDOLF SIEBERT was born in Frankfurt aM, Germany, in 1927. He studied theology, philosophy, philology and history at the Universities of Mainz and Münster, Germany, and at the Catholic University of America, Washington, DC, USA. He has widely taught and lectured in Europe, the USA and Canada. From 1962-65, he taught sociology, economics and theology at St Agnes and Loyola College in Baltimore, Maryland. Since 1965, Siebert has been professor of religion and society in the Religion Department of Western Michigan University, Kalamazoo, Michigan. In 1978-79 he was visiting professor at Kings College, Western Ontario University, London, Ontario, Canada. In the last three decades, Siebert has concentrated his teaching, lecturing and writing in Europe and North America on the philosophy of G. W. F. Hegel, the Frankfurt school of philosophy and sociology, and critical political theology. In 1977 he initiated and has since directed the international course on *The Future of Religion: Source, Product or Negation of Alienation* in the Inter-University Centre of Post-Graduate Studies in Dubrovnik, Yugoslavia. He is founder of *The Centre for Humanistic Future Studies* at Western Michigan University. His main works are: *From Critical Theory of Society to Theology of Communicative Praxis*; *Hegel's Philosophy of History: Theological, Humanistic, Scientific Elements*; *Hegel's Concept of Marriage and Family: Subjective Freedom*; and *Horkheimer's Critical Sociology of Religion: The Relative and the Transcendent* (1979). Rudolf and Margaret Siebert are the parents of seven children.

CARL STARKLOFF received his first degree at St Louis University and a PhD at the University of Ottawa. He has just ceased being director and pastor of St Stephen's Indian Mission, Wind River Indian Reservation, Wyoming, USA, and is at present a member of the faculty of Regis College (Jesuit School of Theology), Toronto, Ontario, Canada, for work in missiology and native ministry formation. His writings include *The Office of Proclamation in the Theology of Karl Barth* (Ottawa 1969) and *People of the Center: American Indian Religion and Christianity* (New York 1974) as well as some thirty-five articles, most of them on missiology or American Indians, in such journals as the *Journal of Ecumenical Studies, Theological Studies, Missiology, Christian Century* and *Occasional Bulletin of Missionary Research*.

CONCILIUM

Claude Geffré. 0 8164 2542 6 144pp.

87. **The Future of Christian Marriage.** Ed. William Bassett and Peter Huizing.
0 8164 2575 2.

88. **Polarization in the Church.** Ed. Hans Küng and Walter Kasper.
0 8164 2572 8 156pp.

89. **Spiritual Revivals.** Ed. Christian Duquoc and Casiano Floristán.
0 8164 2573 6 156pp.

90. **Power and the Word of God.** Ed. Franz Bockle and Jacques Marie Pohier.
0 8164 2574 4 156pp.

91. **The Church as Institution.** Ed. Gregory Baum and Andrew Greeley. 0 8164 2575 2 168pp.

92. **Politics and Liturgy.** Ed. Herman Schmidt and David Power. 0 8164 2576 0 156pp.

93. **Jesus Christ and Human Freedom.** Ed. Edward Schillebeeckx and Bas van Iersel. 0 8164 2577 9 168pp.

94. **The Experience of Dying.** Ed. Norbert Greinacher and Alois Müller. 0 8164 2578 7 156pp.

95. **Theology of Joy.** Ed. Johannes Baptist Metz and Jean-Pierre Jossua. 0 8164 2579 5 164pp.

96. **The Mystical and Political Dimension of the Christian Faith.** Ed. Claude Geffré and Gustavo Guttierez.
0 8164 2580 9 168pp.

97. **The Future of the Religious Life.** Ed. Peter Huizing and William Bassett. 0 8164 2094 7 96pp.

98. **Christians and Jews.** Ed. Hans Küng and Walter Kasper.
0 8164 2095 5 96pp.

99. **Experience of the Spirit.** Ed. Peter Huizing and William Bassett. 0 8164 2096 3 144pp.

100. **Sexuality in Contemporary Catholicism.** Ed. Franz Bockle and Jacques Marie Pohier.
0 8164 2097 1 126pp.

101. **Ethnicity.** Ed. Andrew Greeley and Gregory Baum.
0 8164 2145 5 120pp.

102. **Liturgy and Cultural Religious Traditions.** Ed. Herman Schmidt and David Power. 0 8164 2146 2 120pp.

103. **A Personal God?** Ed. Edward Schillebeeckx and Bas van Iersel. 0 8164 2149 8 142pp.

104. **The Poor and the Church.** Ed. Norbert Greinacher and Alois Müller. 0 8164 2147 1 128pp.

105. **Christianity and Socialism.** Ed. Johannes Baptist Metz and Jean-Pierre Jossua.
0 8164 2148 X 144pp.

106. **The Churches of Africa: Future Prospects.** Ed. Claude Geffré and Bertrand Luneau.
0 8164 2150 1 128pp.

107. **Judgement in the Church.** Ed. William Bassett and Peter Huizing. 0 8164 2166 8 128pp.

108. **Why Did God Make Me?** Ed. Hans Küng and Jürgen Moltmann. 0 8164 2167 6 112pp.

109. **Charisms in the Church.** Ed. Christian Duquoc and Casiano Floristán. 0 8164 2168 4 128pp.

110. **Moral Formation and Christianity.** Ed. Franz Bockle and Jacques Marie Pohier.
0 8164 2169 2 120pp.

111. **Communication in the Church.** Ed. Gregory Baum and Andrew Greeley. 0 8164 2170 6 126pp.

112. **Liturgy and Human Passage.** Ed. David Power and Luis Maldonado. 0 8164 2608 2 136pp.

113. **Revelation and Experience.** Ed. Edward Schillebeeckx and Bas van Iersel. 0 8164 2609 0 134pp.

114. **Evangelization in the World Today.** Ed. Norbert Greinacher and Alois Müller. 0 8164 2610 4 136pp.

115. **Doing Theology in New Places.** Ed. Jean-Pierre Jossua and Johannes Baptist Metz.
0 8164 2611 2 120pp.

116. **Buddhism and Christianity.** Ed. Claude Geffré and Mariasusai Dhavamony. 0 8164 2612 0 136pp.

117. **The Finances of the Church.** Ed. William Bassett and Peter Huizing. 0 8164 2197 8 160pp.

118. **An Ecumenical Confession of Faith?** Ed. Hans Küng and Jürgen Moltmann. 0 8164 2198 6 136pp.

119. **Discernment of the Spirit and of Spirits.** Ed. Casiano Floristán and Christian Duquoc.
0 8164 2199 4 136pp.

120. **The Death Penalty and Torture.** Ed. Franz Bockle and Jacques Marie Pohier. 0 8164 2200 1 136pp.

121. **The Family in Crisis or in Transition.** Ed. Andrew Greely.
0 567 30001 3 128pp.

122. **Structures of Initiation in Crisis.** Ed. Luis Maldonado and David Power. 0 567 30002 1 128pp.

123. **Heaven.** Ed. Bas van Iersel and Edward Schillebeeckx.
0 567 30003 X 120pp.

124. **The Church and the Rights of Man.** Ed. Alois Müller and Norbert Greinacher.
0 567 30004 8 140pp.

125. **Christianity and the Bourgeoisie.** Ed. Johannes Baptist Metz.
0 567 30005 6 144pp.

126. **China as a Challenge to the Church.** Ed. Claude Geffré and Joseph Spae. 0 567 30006 4 136pp.

127. **The Roman Curia and the Communion of Churches.** Ed. Peter Huizing and Knut Walf.
0 567 30007 2 144pp.

128. **Conflicts about the Holy Spirit.** Ed. Hans Küng and Jürgen Moltmann 0 567 30008 0 144pp.

129. **Models of Holiness.** Ed. Christian Duquoc and Casiano Floristán.
0 567 30009 9 128pp.

130. **The Dignity of the Despised of the Earth.** Ed. Jacques Marie

Pohier and Dietmar Mieth. 0 567 30010 2 144pp.

131. **Work and Religion.** Ed. Gregory Baum. 0 567 30011 0 148pp.

132. **Symbol and Art in Worship.** Ed. Luis Maldonado and David Power. 0 567 30012 9 136pp.

133. **Right of the Community to a Priest.** Ed. Edward Schillebeeckx and Johannes Baptist Metz. 0 567 30013 7 148pp.

134. **Women in a Men's Church.** Ed. Virgil Elizondo and Norbert Greinacher. 0 567 30014 5 144pp.

135. **True and False Universality of Christianity.** Ed. Claude Geffré and Jean-Pierre Jossua.
0 567 30015 3 138pp.

136. **What is Religion? An Inquiry for Christian Theology.** Ed. Mircea Eliade and David Tracy.
0 567 30016 1 98pp.

137. **Electing our Own Bishops.** Ed. Peter Huizing and Knut Walf.
0 567 30017 X 112pp.

138. **Conflicting Ways of Interpreting the Bible.** Ed. Hans Küng and Jürgen Moltmann. 0 567 30018 8 112pp.

139. **Christian Obedience.** Ed. Casiano Floristán and Christian Duquoc. 0 567 30019 6 96pp.

140. **Christian Ethics and Economics: the North-South Conflict.** Ed. Dietmar Mieth and Jacques Marie Pohier. 0 567 30020 X 128pp.

1981

141. **Neo-Conservatism: Social and Religious Phenomenon.** Ed. Gregory Baum and John Coleman. 0 567 30021 8.

142. **The Times of Celebration.** Ed. David Power and Mary Collins.
0 567 30022 6.

143. **God as Father.** Ed. Edward Schillebeeckx and Johannes Baptist Metz. 0 567 30023 4.

144. **Tensions Between the Churches of the First World and the Third World.** Ed. Virgil Elizondo and Norbert Greinacher.
0 567 30024 2.

145. **Nietzsche and Christianity.** Ed. Claude Geffré and Jean-Pierre Jossua. 0 567 30025 0.

146. **Where Does the Church Stand?** Ed. Giuseppe Alberigo.
0 567 30026 9.

147. **The Revised Code of Canon Law: a Missed Opportunity?** Ed. Peter Huizing and Knut Walf.
0 567 30027 7.

148. **Who Has the Say in the Church?** Ed. Hans Küng and Jürgen Moltmann. 0 567 30028 5.

149. **Francis of Assisi Today.** Ed. Casiano Floristán and Christian Duquoc.
0 567 30029 3.

150. **Christian Ethics: Uniformity, Universality, Pluralism.** Ed. Jacques Pohier and Dietmar Mieth. 0 567 30030 7.

All back issues are still in print and available for sale. Orders should be sent to the publishers,

T. & T. CLARK LIMITED

36 George Street, Edinburgh EH2 2LQ, Scotland